POWER FROM ON HIGH

Power from on High

The Holy Spirit in the Gospels and Acts

Salvador Carrillo Alday, M.Sp.S.

Translated by Carolyn Mishler

SERVANT BOOKS
Ann Arbor, Michigan

Translation copyright © 1978 by Servant Books

Published by: Servant Books
P.O. Box 8617
Ann Arbor, Michigan 48107

Available from: Servant Publications
Distribution Center
237 North Michigan
South Bend, Indiana 46601

Originally published in 1977 as *El Espiritu Santo*
Copyright © 1977 by Salvador Carrillo Alday

The present bibliography has been revised and enlarged by the author.

Scripture quotations in this book are from *The Jerusalem Bible,* copyright © 1966 by Darton, Longman & Todd, Ltd. and Doubleday & Company, Inc. and used by permission of the publisher.

Printed in the United States of America

ISBN 0-89283-060-3

CONTENTS

Introduction / vii

I. *The Gospels: The Holy Spirit in the Mystery of Jesus*
   1. The Conception and Infancy of Jesus / 3
   2. The Messianic Anointing of Jesus / 13
   3. Jesus, Led by the Spirit / 19
   4. The Teaching of Jesus on the Holy Spirit / 30
   5. The Gift of the Spirit / 60
   6. "In the Name of the Father and of the Son and of the Holy Spirit" / 68

II. *Acts of the Apostles: The Holy Spirit in the Church*
   7. The Dawning of the Church / 73
   8. The First Communities / 94
   9. The Great Missions / 109

Bibliography / 131

INTRODUCTION

On the last day of the week-long feast of Tabernacles, the greatest day of the celebration, Jesus stood up in the Temple and shouted:

> If any man is thirsty, let him come to me! Let the man come and drink who believes in me! (Jn 7:37b)

The evangelist comments on this enigmatic phrase, saying:

> As scripture says: From his breast shall flow fountains of living water. He was speaking of the Spirit which those who believed in him were to receive; for there was no Spirit as yet because Jesus had not yet been glorified. (Jn 7:37-39)

Yes, the gift of the Spirit of God which was promised for messianic times was reserved to Jesus, the Messiah; but not until Jesus had been perfectly glorified by his Father.

Jesus wants to give us his Spirit even now, and if we are thirsty for this, how much more must Jesus be thirsty for it! These pages have been written so that you may better know and love the Spirit of God, the Holy Spirit, promised by the Father and sent into the world by him and by Jesus.

This book is divided into two parts. The first, entitled *The Holy Spirit in the Mystery of Jesus,* explains all the gospel passages which concern the Holy Spirit. This part is divided into six chapters.

The first chapter presents the people involved in the accounts of Matthew and Luke of the conception and infancy of Jesus:

Mary, Zechariah, Elizabeth, John the Baptist, and Simeon. All of them appear as "full of the Holy Spirit," always acting under the impulse of his prompting.

The second chapter is devoted to the messianic anointing of Jesus at the Jordan as described in the synoptic gospels. This was a surpassingly important moment in the life of Jesus, since, according to God's plan, this anointing would mark the beginning of Jesus' apostolic mission. Jesus the Messiah is manifested as the Son of God, who, like another Moses, Lawgiver and Prophet, will bring forth the new people of God, the messianic people.

The third chapter shows us Jesus in full public ministry. It shows how he is enlightened, moved, and guided always by the power of the Spirit to establish the kingdom of heaven on earth. It is drawn from the synoptic accounts.

The fourth chapter, the longest, gives us the teachings of Jesus about the Holy Spirit. These come to us from the Gospel of John, from pages resplendent with light and doctrine, which the evangelist could write only by the enlightenment of the divine Spirit.

The fifth chapter treats of the gift of the Spirit as recorded in the Gospel of John. The evangelist, with all discretion but with sufficient clarity, twice announces the gift of the Spirit in describing the scene of the crucifixion. We see this in the "I thirst" of Jesus at the moment in which he gives up his Spirit and dies, and in the water that springs forth from his pierced side. The evangelist proclaims the gift of the spirit with great solemnity in writing about the afternoon of Easter day when Jesus appeared to his disciples, breathed on them and said, "Receive the Holy Spirit!"

The sixth chapter seeks to explain the final passage in the Gospel of Matthew, where the liturgical formula for Christian baptism is found: "Go, therefore, make disciples of all the nations; baptize them in the name of the Father and of the Son and of the Holy Spirit" (Mt 28:19).

The second part of this book is called *Acts of the Apostles: The Holy Spirit in the Church*. It is devoted to the study of the many texts offered us by Luke concerning the action of the Holy Spirit in the apostolic church. There are three chapters.

The first chapter presents the Holy Spirit giving life to the mother church in Jerusalem. The heart and culmination of the Book of Acts is, without doubt, the charismatic outpouring of the Holy Spirit on the day of Pentecost.

In the second chapter we see the Holy Spirit acting powerfully in the communities of Palestine and Damascus.

In the third chapter the Holy Spirit shines as the soul of the great evangelistic enterprises. The same Holy Spirit that has filled Jesus now descends and anoints the missionaries of the good news, taking possession of them and leading them from Jerusalem to the capital of the empire—Rome, the end of the earth—to bear witness to Jesus.

The Holy Spirit is the soul which instilled life into the early church. And may that Holy Spirit, to whom these pages are consecrated, fall in fullness upon us and interiorly transform us. May he fulfill, to the glory of the Father, the promise made through the prophet Isaiah:

I will pour my Spirit on your descendants,
my blessing on your children.
They shall grow like grass where there is plenty of water, like poplars by running streams. (Is 44:3b-4)

Part I

The Gospels: The Holy Spirit in the Mystery of Jesus

CHAPTER ONE

THE CONCEPTION AND INFANCY OF JESUS

Gospel of Matthew

The Virginal Conception of Jesus and the Mission of Joseph (Mt 1:18-20)

> This is how Jesus Christ came to be born. His mother Mary was betrothed to Joseph; but before they came to live together she was found to be with child through the Holy Spirit. (1:18)

Matthew reveals all at once the mystery of the conception of Jesus, the Messiah. Whether she was already married, or perhaps only engaged, Mary did not live with Joseph. In these circumstances "she was found to be with child through the Holy Spirit." The passive form "was found" shows the unexpected character and divine origin of the conception. It also expresses a note of wonder and surprise.

The virginal conception of Jesus is clearly affirmed in these words. Mary did not conceive by the work of any man; her conception was by a sovereign act of God and by his power.

By the time of the writing of the gospel, the expression "Holy Spirit" had acquired its full meaning as the Holy Spirit sent by the Father through the glorified Jesus.

Her husband Joseph, being a man of honor and wanting to spare her publicity, decided to divorce her informally. (1:19)

According to biblical tradition, a "man of honor" or a "just man" (another possible translation) is a man who is virtuous (Gn 6:9). For the contemporaries of the evangelist, the just man is not the avenger without pity, but rather the man who, while respecting his neighbor and human feelings, devotes himself to the good of all, particularly the lowly (Wis 12:19; Ps 37:21).

Therefore, the adjective "just" as used here draws attention to the balance of Joseph's judgment and the deliberation which preceded his decision. Faced with the fact that his wife had conceived without his cooperation, Joseph carefully considers the situation and adopts the best solution: one of discretion and mercy.

Desiring, then, to safeguard the reputation of his wife, Joseph refuses to denounce her and plans to separate from her secretly. This merciful decision reveals not only his wisdom and self-control, but great kindness, generous mercy, and largeness of soul. The justice of Joseph is a faithfulness to the Law, cloaked in active and humble piety which culminates in a concrete gesture of mercy.

Joseph does not want to divorce Mary informally because he wishes to respectfully retire from her after learning of the marvel of the virginal conception. Nor does he want to divorce Mary because, convinced of her virtue, he is reluctant to give over to the rigors of the Law a mystery he does not understand (see Dt 22:20). On the contrary, it is because he does suspect the faithfulness of his wife that he seeks to quietly divorce her. It is precisely for this reason that the angel intervenes.

The angel of the Lord appears to Joseph in a dream, saying:

Joseph son of David, do not be afraid to take Mary home as your wife, because she has conceived what is in her by the Holy Spirit. She will give birth to a son and you must name him Jesus, because he is the one who is to save his people from their sins. (1:20b–21)

The angel reveals to Joseph the miraculous conception that took place by the power of the Spirit of God in Mary's womb. As at the dawn of creation, when life burst forth into the universe through the action of the Spirit of God which hovered over the primitive chaos (Gn 1:2), so now, life has become present in Mary's womb thanks to the fruitful action of the Holy Spirit. In this way the angel calms Joseph and invites him to receive Mary into his home.

Verse 21 is important. Mary is going to give birth to a son, but it is Joseph who should name the infant (Gn 17:19). In the biblical mentality, to give a name meant to take possession of the person named (Gn 2:19; 2 Kgs 24:17). Even more, this choice of a name was seen as determining beforehand the person's mission (Gn 2:20; 17:5, 15ff; Jn 1:42). Thus Joseph, on obeying the divine order to give a name to the child, takes possession of him and is established as his father. By calling him *Jesus,* which means *Yahweh saves,* Joseph destines his son from that first moment for his fundamental saving mission. This is brought out by the words of the angel, "He is the one who is to save his people from their sins."

From the beginning, the Gospel of Matthew places the messiahship of Jesus in an especially religious line. His mission will be *spiritual.* Israel is his people, and he will save them from their sins. A purely national and political messiahship is outside the horizons of this key text.

Gospel of Luke

John the Baptist: Prophet Anointed by the Holy Spirit

> The angel said to him, "Zechariah, do not be afraid, your prayer has been heard. Your wife Elizabeth is to bear you a son and you must name him John. He will be your joy and delight and many will rejoice at his birth, for he will be great in the sight of the Lord; he must drink no wine, no strong drink. Even from his mother's womb he will be filled with the Holy Spirit, and he will bring back many of the sons of Israel to the Lord their God. With the spirit and power of Elijah, he will go before him to turn the hearts of fathers toward their children and the disobedient back to the wisdom that the virtuous have, preparing for the Lord a people fit for him." (1:13–17)

These verses describe the mission of John the Baptist. They are the heart of the account in which Luke describes John's birth. Numerous prophetic utterances are to be fulfilled in John's life.

The angel begins by telling Zechariah, "Do not be afraid, your prayer has been heard." The expression "Do not be afraid" is very common in the Old Testament; it is used to impart peace and security before a special intervention of God (Gn 15:1; 26:24; 46:3).

Perhaps in his prayer Zechariah did not ask for a son; this could account for his spontaneous reaction, "I am an old man and my wife is getting on in years" (1:18). The request to which the angel refers was probably the prayer for messianic salvation which the priest—Zechariah in this case—raises to God in the name of all the people during his service in the Temple. God heard this petition and will therefore give Zechariah and his wife a son, in spite of their advanced age. Through him will begin the realization of the promises.

As it appears in other annunciations in the Bible the father is the one who gives his son a name (Gn 17:19). He will be called John, which means "Yahweh is gracious."

The birth of the boy will be a cause of joy and happiness. It is a messianic joy, a favorite theme of this evangelist (1:18, 44, 47; 2:10).

John will be great before the Lord. He will be the crowning figure among all the great servants of God who went before him:

1. He will be a Nazarene, that is, one consecrated to the Lord like Samson and Samuel (Nm 6:3-4; Jgs 13:4, 7, 14; 1 Sm 1:11).

2. John will be full of the Holy Spirit from his mother's womb. He will be a true prophet—in the same way as Jeremiah and the Servant of Yahweh—and anointed as such from before birth (Jer 1:5; Is 49:1). As all the prophets were chosen by the Spirit, it was fitting that the prophet who would point out the Messiah be consecrated by the Spirit of God in an even more excellent way. John was therefore filled with the Spirit from his mother's womb (1 Kgs 18:12; Ez 3:12; 8:3; 11:1; Jer 1:5; Is 49:1).

3. John's mission will be that of converting his brothers to the Lord his God, as was the case with Levi (Mal 2:6).

4. John will be the precursor of God and will have the spirit, the power, and the zeal of God in the manner of Elijah (Mal 3:1, 23–24; Sir 48:10; Mt 17:11–13).

5. John will prepare for the Lord a people, thus fulfilling the prophecy of Is 40:3.

And John truly was great. Jesus himself affirmed it when he said, "Of all the children born of women, there is no one greater than John" (Lk 7:28a).

"The Holy Spirit Will Come Upon You" (Lk 1:35–37)

> "The Holy Spirit will come upon you" the angel answered "and the power of the Most High will cover you with its shadow. And so the child will be holy and will be called Son of God. Know this too: your kinswoman Elizabeth has, in her old age, herself conceived a son, and she whom people called barren is now in her sixth month, for nothing is impossible to God." (1:35–37)

Here is found the essential element of the dialogue between the Virgin Mary and the angel (1:28–38), and the summit of the theological exposition of the evangelist. The sovereign and fruitful action of the Spirit of God, in itself mysterious and inexpressible, which will make Mary able to conceive and give birth to the Messiah (1:31–33), is described by two vigorous images taken from the Old Testament.

1. *The Holy Spirit will come upon you.* The outpouring of the Spirit of God upon a person in order to accomplish a saving work through him, is frequently found in scripture (Nm 11:25–29; 1 Sm 10:6, 10; 16:13; Is 32:15; 42:1; 61:1). In the conception of the Messiah, the Son of the Most High, it is to be expected that the Spirit of God will act in all his power.

2. *The power of the Most High will cover you with its shadow.* This expression is less frequent than the former and therefore more significant. "Cover with his shadow" is a figure that recalls the cloud that filled the Tabernacle in the Old Testament (Ex 40:35). It is also a symbol of the protection which God offers to those who

cling to him. God is likened to a bird which covers her eggs with her wings and later gathers her offspring to herself (Ps 9:4; 140:8). This evokes the image of the creator Spirit at the origin of the world, who, like a bird which incubates her eggs so that life can come forth from them, hovered over the waters at creation and brought forth life in all the varieties pronounced by the divine Word (Gn 1:2).

Here the Holy Spirit, the Power of the Most High, is going to cover Mary with his shadow so that a new life can burst forth within her. Through these expressions the evangelist clearly wants to show that the Spirit will play the role of principal creator and will himself produce the life in Mary's womb. That which the Spirit, God's creative breath, has done since the foundation of the world, he is going to do now in a virgin by effecting in her a virginal conception. In the conception of Jesus everything comes from the power of the Spirit.

As the result of the creative action of the Spirit in Mary's womb, "the child will be holy and will be called Son of God."

A faithful examination of both text and context reveals that the title "Son of God" has immense significance in the eyes of Luke, and is the object of his theological purposes. The angel had said in the first part of the message that the child would be called "Son of the Most High" in the messianic sense (1:31–33). Now, in the second part, Luke shows that the title "Son of God" will receive a totally new and higher meaning because of the virginal conception. The virginal conception is a perceptible sign that manifests an article of faith: Jesus is Son of God by special, unique, exclusive right. The evangelist instills in this title the full content of his Christian faith.

A further consideration: Adam, like Jesus, had no earthly father. This being so, Adam was head of the race; Jesus will also be head of the race. He is a new Adam, a new man. He is a point of departure, for with him begins a new generation, a new humanity.

The angel gives Mary a sign: Elizabeth's conception of a child in her old age. The purpose of this sign is not to strengthen Mary's faith, but rather to fulfill a law of biblical annunciations (Jgs 6:36–

40; Is 7:10–16). The angel's message sets the scene for the visitation (1:39ff).

"Elizabeth Was Filled with the Holy Spirit" (Lk 1:41–45)

Now as soon as Elizabeth heard Mary's greeting, the child leaped in her womb and Elizabeth was filled with the Holy Spirit. She gave a loud cry and said, "Of all women you are the most blessed, and blessed is the fruit of your womb. Why should I be honored with a visit from the mother of my Lord? For the moment your greeting reached my ears, the child in my womb leaped for joy. Yes, blessed is she who believed that the promise made her by the Lord would be fulfilled." (1:41–45)

In this passage, which depicts a messianic scene, Luke goes immediately to the essentials. We notice that two effects follow upon Mary's greeting:

1. The child leaps for joy in the womb of his mother. This leap is an expression of messianic joy. The Greek verb used by the evangelist recalls Ps 114:4, 6; Wis 19:9; and Mal 3:20. It is at this moment that the announcement of the angel in Lk 1:15 is fulfilled. The child is consecrated as a prophet and anointed by the Spirit for the mission that is going to be entrusted to him.

2. Elizabeth, as well as her future child, was filled with the Holy Spirit. Anointed by the Spirit, she can now speak a prophetic word. The expression "gave a loud cry" serves not merely to indicate the tone of voice, but the importance of the words.

a) Elizabeth blesses Mary and her child. This greeting recalls the blessings of Dt 28:4; Jgs 5:24; and Jdt 13:18.

b) Elizabeth recognizes the child conceived in Mary's womb as her Lord. The evangelist often gives the title of "Lord" to Jesus during his earthly life (Lk 7:13; 10:1, 39, 41; 11:39; 12:42).

The joyful leap of the child in Elizabeth's womb is like a greeting to the Messiah in Mary's womb. While the scene is that of the meeting of two future mothers, above all it is the meeting of the Precursor and the Messiah.

c) The Virgin Mary is declared a believer of God's word and therefore is called blessed. Luke underlines a contrast here: While Zechariah lacked faith (1:20), Mary, on the other hand, believed. In Elizabeth there also shines a great faith. She has been receptive to the signs and is convinced that all that God has said will be fulfilled in Mary.

"Zechariah Was Filled with the Holy Spirit and Spoke this Prophecy" (Lk 1:67)

On the day of his son's circumcision, Zechariah is questioned concerning what name the child should receive. He writes on a tablet: "John." At that moment Zechariah miraculously regains his speech and immediately breaks forth into a blessing of God.

> His father Zechariah was filled with the Holy Spirit and spoke this prophecy: "Blessed be the Lord, the God of Israel ..." (1:67–68a)

Like Elizabeth, Zechariah is also filled with the Holy Spirit and is moved to prophesy. His prophecy is above all a song of thanks to the Lord, the God of Israel, for the messianic salvation, the saving plan of God (1:68–79).

The Canticle of Zechariah, also called the Benedictus, parallels Mary's Magnificat. It is a poetic piece which probably had its origin in Jewish piety or the primitive Christian community in Jerusalem. Luke has retouched this "psalm," and placed it on the lips of Zechariah.

Simeon, Man of the Spirit (Lk 2:25–32)

> Now in Jerusalem there was a man named Simeon. He was an upright and devout man; he looked forward to Israel's comforting and the Holy Spirit rested on him. It had been revealed to him by the Holy Spirit that he would not see death until he had set eyes on the Christ of the Lord. Prompted by the Spirit he

came to the Temple; and when the parents brought in the child Jesus to do for him what the Law required, he took him into his arms and blessed God. (2:25-28)

Luke paints a portrait of this man and highlights four specific features:
1. The adjectives "upright" and "devout" show Simeon to be a man of integrity in the moral and religious realm.
2. The expression "looked forward to Israel's comforting" has roots especially in the prophet Isaiah. It is the equivalent of saying that Simeon was a man of faith and was waiting for the salvation promised by God to his people Israel (Is 40:1; 49:13; 51:12; 61:2).
3. The phrase "the Holy Spirit rested on him" underscores the enduring quality of the Spirit's presence with this just man. In addition, the traditional, biblical choice of words indicates that Simeon was a prophet (Nm 11:17, 25, 29; 2 Kgs 2:15; Is 11:2; 42:1; 61:1; Ez 11:5). As a matter of fact, he had received a revelation from the Spirit: "He would not see death until he had set eyes on the Christ of the Lord." "The Christ" refers to the Messiah of God, the Anointed of Yahweh (Ex 30:22; 1 Sm 24:7, 11; 26:9, 11, 16, 23; 2 Sm 1:14, 16; Ps 2:7; 16:10; 110:4, 6).
4. This revelation of the Holy Spirit to Simeon is important. It shows the extent of Simeon's prophetic charism and places him among the great ones sent by God. If to receive even in an obscure way the announcement of the Messiah was an important charismatic gift in such prophets as Isaiah, Jeremiah, Micah, and others, how much greater the grace for Simeon to receive the promise of seeing the Messiah during his own life and to enjoy the fulfillment of that promise! Since God had sent a whole series of prophets to announce the coming of the Messiah, it is not strange that at his appearance God himself would bring forth new prophets who would indicate his presence in the midst of the people.

Prompted by the Spirit, Simeon went to the Temple; and when the parents presented the child Jesus to fulfill what the Law prescribed for him, the prophet took him in his arms and blessed God, saying:

Now, Master, you can let your servant go in peace, just as you promised; because my eyes have seen the salvation which you have prepared for all the nations to see, a light to enlighten the pagans and the glory of your people Israel. (2:29-32)

To bless God is to praise him, to glorify him, to exalt him. Simeon's blessing is inspired by the action of the Holy Spirit, once again, who rests upon him.

It is noteworthy that the evangelist has mentioned the Holy Spirit three times in relation to Simeon. Simeon was a man of the Spirit.

CHAPTER TWO

THE MESSIANIC ANOINTING OF JESUS

I baptize you in water for repentance, but the one who follows me ... will baptize you with the Holy Spirit and fire. (Mt 3:11)

The Baptism of John

John, anointed as prophet by the Holy Spirit from his mother's womb, appeared in the desert of Judah proclaiming a baptism of repentance for the forgiveness of sins (Mk 1:4; 3:3). This repentance or conversion had as its objective the preparing of hearts for the coming of the Lord, so fulfilling the promises made by God through the prophets (Is 40:3–5; Mal 3:1).

John baptized. "To baptize," derived from *bapto,* which means "to wash," refers specifically to the act of submerging in water with the purpose of purifying. In regard to the baptism of John the sense of the verb is literal: John baptized people in water by submerging them in water.

Nevertheless, this exterior action symbolized something even more important. The people went to John "and as they were baptized by him in the river Jordan they confessed their sins" (Mt 3:6). John baptized in water for repentance so that men might abandon sin and return to God. The baptism in water offered by John was an external sign of interior purification, the fruit of conversion.

The Baptism of the Messiah.

In the case of the messianic baptism, the purification will be much more radical and perfect. The purifying element will not only be water but "the Holy Spirit and fire."

The expression "in the Holy Spirit and fire" can be translated "in the fire of the Spirit," indicating the profound purification wrought by the Spirit of God. The Holy Spirit washes, cleans, and purifies as deeply and radically as fire purifies metals.

It is this perspective that leads John the Baptist to describe the work of the Messiah according to the forceful images of the great prophets:

> See, the name of Yahweh comes from afar, blazing in his anger, heavy his exaction. His lips brim with fury, his tongue is like a devouring fire. His breath is like a river in spate coming up to the neck. (Is 30:27–28a; compare Is 30:28b–33; 41:15–16; 66:24; Jer 7:30–8:3; 19:1–13)

Nevertheless, the gospel expression "He will baptize you with the Holy Spirit and fire" is already shaped by a Christian perspective. By itself, this expression could refer to Christian baptism (1 Cor 6:11; Ti 3:5). Because of the allusion to fire, however, perhaps it is accurate also to refer the expression to the charismatic outpouring of the Holy Spirit on Pentecost (Acts 1:5; 2:1–4).

Peter's words on the day of Pentecost clearly indicate that the gift of the Spirit is linked very closely to conversion and baptism: "You must repent . . . and everyone of you must be baptized in the name of Jesus Christ for the forgiveness of your sins, and you will receive the gift of the Holy Spirit" (Acts 2:38; see also Acts 10:44–48; 11:16).

In brief, the expression "He will baptize you in the Holy Spirit and fire" is a fundamental one, and sums up the messianic work of Jesus.

The Anointing of Jesus in the Jordan (Mk 1:10–11; Mt 3:16–17; Lk 3:21–22; Jn 1:32–33)

> No sooner had he come up out of the water than he saw the heavens torn apart and the Spirit, like a dove, descending on him. And a voice came from heaven, "You are my Son, the Beloved; my favor rests on you." (Mk 1:10–11)

The synoptic evangelists place this theophany immediately after the baptism of Jesus. This means that with the baptism of Jesus an epoch has ended and a new era has begun, the messianic era. The fourth evangelist does not tell the story of Jesus' baptism, but only alludes to it.

Luke's account of the baptism of Jesus notes that Jesus was praying at the moment when the heavens opened. Throughout his Gospel Luke is eager to present Jesus as often being in intimate communication with his Father (5:16; 6:12; 9:18, 28–29; 10:21; 11:1; 22:32, 40–46; 23:34, 46).

The phrase "No sooner had he come up out of the water . . ." recalls the text of Is 63:11 which describes Moses, the pastor of the flock of Israel, whom God brought out of the waters of the sea (Ex 2:1), and on whom he put his Holy Spirit (Nm 11:17).

> They remembered the days of old, of Moses his servant. Where is he who brought out of the sea the shepherd of his flock? Where is he who endowed him with his holy spirit . . .? (Is 63:11)

The expression "He saw the heavens torn apart and the Spirit . . descending on him" recalls another verse from the same poem of Isaiah, namely, "Oh, that you would tear the heavens open and come down . . ." (Is 63:19b).

In the Gospel of Mark it is Jesus who "saw." This is a matter, then, of Jesus' own personal experience. The expression "descending on him" in the original Greek indicates that the Spirit not only comes down on Jesus, but enters into him.

By means of this series of allusions Mark discreetly presents the beginning of Jesus' public ministry as being similar to the beginning of the public life of Moses. Mark is showing that Jesus will be head of a new holy people.

Matthew, followed by Luke, evokes scenes of the prophet Ezekiel on the banks of the Kebar River (Ez 1:1): "Heaven opened and I saw . . ." and "the spirit came into me . . ." (Ez 2:2). "Heaven opened" is an image which signifies a revelation from God and a communication between earth and heaven (Jn 1:51; Acts 7:56; 10:11–16; Rv 4:1; 19:11).

Matthew wants to show that Jesus is the new Prophet, full of the Spirit; and that like Ezekiel, Jesus will be sent in the power of the Spirit to perform a mission among the people of Israel (Ez 2:3).

The Holy Spirit is symbolized as a dove. This image probably has its origin in the image of the Spirit of God hovering over the waters of creation (Gn 1:2). At this moment in Jesus' life a new creation is breaking forth thanks to the power of the Spirit.

> And a voice came from heaven, "You are my Son, the Beloved; my favor rests on you." (Mk 1:11)

The first phrase "You are my Son, the Beloved" is a reference to Gn 22:2 where Abraham receives from God the order to sacrifice Isaac: "Take your son . . . your only son, Isaac, whom you love, and go to the land of Moriah. There you shall offer him as a burnt offering, on a mountain I will point out to you" (see also Gn 22:12, 16).

The second phrase "My favor rests on you" together with the gift of the Spirit is a clear allusion to one of Isaiah's oracles describing the Servant of Yahweh:

> Here is my servant whom I uphold, my chosen one in whom my soul delights. I have endowed him with my spirit that he may bring true justice to the nations. (Is 42:1)

From this perspective, the voice coming from heaven shows that Jesus is like Isaac, whose sacrifice had been asked of Abraham by God. At the same time, the voice shows that Jesus is like the Servant of Yahweh, who, being the object of divine favor and full of the Holy Spirit, has a messianic mission to fulfill.

The theological meaning of the whole scene is of the greatest importance. In the time of Jesus the messianic hope was frequently formulated with reference to three passages in the Book of Isaiah which announced the coming of the Spirit of God upon the Liberator of Israel (Is 11:1-2; 42:1; 61:1). This messianic liberation was conceived of as a new Exodus, a new passing through the Red Sea (Is 11:15-16; 43:16-21; 51:10; 63:11-13).

Therefore, the primary sense of the scene is the following: When Jesus sees that the Holy Spirit is descending upon him, and hears the heavenly voice which tells him that he is the "Beloved Son" and the "Servant" in whom Yahweh is pleased, Jesus finds out, or receives confirmation, that he is the one chosen by God to bring about the liberation of his people. He is like a new Moses, a new Servant of Yahweh, and even more, he is like a new Isaac, son of the promise.

Nevertheless, it is clear that Jesus is not just a simple copy or a rich synthesis of the important figures in biblical history. By means of these allusions the Bible authors, and through them the Holy Spirit who inspired them, wish to show us that Jesus will fulfill on a superior level the missions partially entrusted to these earlier personages. Jesus synthesizes these figures and greatly surpasses them. He truly is the Beloved Son, full of the Holy Spirit, in whom the Father takes pleasure.

But how is it possible, one might ask, that Jesus could receive the Spirit of God on the occasion of his baptism? Didn't he possess the fullness of the Spirit from the time of his birth?

To answer this question it is necessary to understand the work that the Spirit was to accomplish in Jesus. According to Is 11:1-2 the Spirit of God is a "spirit of wisdom and insight" given the descendant of David so that he could lead the people of God into the true "knowledge of Yahweh" (Is 11:9; 42:3-4). It is a "spirit of counsel and power" which will enter the Messiah in order to bring about the liberation of Israel, defeating the enemies of his people (see also Is 63:19-64:3a).

Thanks to the Spirit he has just received, Jesus will be able to free the people of God from all the powers of evil. It is not a question, therefore, of the Holy Spirit functioning as the principle of *personal sanctification* for Jesus, but rather of the *charismatic Spirit*, the divine power that acts in Jesus so that he can fulfill the messianic work.

At the Prompting of the Spirit (Mk 1:12; Mt 4:1; Lk 4:1)

Following the events at the Jordan there is a change of course in the life of Jesus. He will not return to Nazareth to take up his ordinary work. Led by the Spirit, who has descended upon him, he will take up a different type of life in order to carry out the mission God his Father entrusted to him.

The description given by Luke is striking:

> Filled with the Holy Spirit, Jesus left the Jordan and was led by the Spirit through the wilderness, being tempted there by the devil for forty days. (4:1–2a)

Jesus is at the disposal of the Spirit who fills him. At the Spirit's urging, Jesus leaves the Jordan, and under his continual leading he spends forty days in the desert. The constant action of the Spirit upon Jesus is expressed in the passive form "was led" employed by the evangelist.

During this time Jesus will undergo the attacks of the Tempter, who wants to dissuade Jesus from the plan set by the Father. But, thanks to the help of the Spirit, Jesus will come out victorious (Mt 4:1–11; Lk 4:1–13).

CHAPTER THREE

JESUS, LED BY THE SPIRIT

"Jesus, with the power of the Spirit in him, returned to Galilee" (Lk 4:14a)

> Jesus, with the power of the Spirit in him, returned to Galilee; and his reputation spread throughout the countryside. He taught in their synagogues and everyone praised him. (4:14–15)

The report of Jesus' return to Galilee is also found in Mark and Matthew (Mk 1:14a; Mt 4:12). Luke emphasizes the fact that Jesus continues his work under the powerful action of the Holy Spirit, the same Spirit who filled him at the Jordan and led him during his stay in the desert. The Spirit acts upon Jesus with divine power.

Moved by the Spirit of God, "a spirit of wisdom and insight, a spirit of counsel and power, a spirit of knowledge and of the fear of Yahweh" (Is 11:2), Jesus began to teach in the synagogues.

The evangelist comments with interest that Jesus' fame spread throughout the entire region and that he was praised by all.

"The Spirit of the Lord Has Been Given to Me" (Lk 4:16–22a)

> He came to Nazara, where he had been brought up, and went into the synagogue on the sabbath day as he usually did. He

stood up to read, and they handed him the scroll of the prophet Isaiah. Unrolling the scroll he found the place where it is written: "The Spirit of the Lord has been given to me, for he has anointed me. He has sent me to bring good news to the poor, to proclaim liberty to captives and to the blind new sight, to set the downtrodden free, to proclaim the Lord's year of favor." He then rolled up the scroll, gave it back to the assistant and sat down. And all eyes in the synagogue were fixed on him. Then he began to speak to them, "This text is being fulfilled today even as you listen." And he won the approval of all, and they were astonished by the gracious words that came from his lips. (4:12–22a)

This story contains elements of the common synoptic tradition (Mk 6:1–6a; Mt 13:54–58), but Luke has retouched it with his own personal genius. Thus he offers us, at the beginning of Jesus' ministry, an inaugural account full of power and majesty.

Nazara is Nazareth, the little town where Jesus spent his childhood, youth, and early manhood. Jesus entered the synagogue there and stood up to read.

The synagogue was the place where the Jews gathered each week to celebrate the sabbath. A portion of the Law and the Prophets was read publicly and an exhortation of some kind was delivered. The right of addressing the assembly in these ways was not limited to the elders of the synagogue. The elders did watch over the service, however, and invited only those versed in scripture to read and teach from it.

Unrolling the scroll, he found the place where it was written . . .

In using the word "found" the evangelist wants to highlight the providential character of this reading, whether it be that Jesus had opened the book at random, or whether the reading followed the established liturgical order. The "place" was a messianic passage from the prophet Isaiah (Is 61:1–2a).

This text originally referred to the author of Is 60–62. Jesus applies it to himself, however, alluding to the fullness of the Spirit he had received at the Jordan and to the evangelizing, liberating mission which, like a "year of favor" for the people, his father had proclaimed, and which was his duty to fulfill.

Luke does not record the content of Jesus' preaching, but affirms that he began to speak as he was rolling up the scroll, saying, "This text is being fulfilled today." Jesus senses that with him has arrived the age of grace announced by the prophet, the "today" of salvation (see also 2:11; 3:22; 5:26; 13:32; 19:9; 23:43).

The result of this first preaching was very positive. Luke comments, "And he won the approval of all, and they were astonished by the gracious words that come from his lips." The teaching of Jesus was full of the divine wisdom that came to him from the Spirit whom he had received at the Jordan (see also Is 11:2).

Jesus, the Servant Full of the Spirit and of Mercy (Mt 12:18)

One sabbath Jesus cured a man who had a paralyzed hand (Mt 12:9–13). The Pharisees reacted by taking counsel together against Jesus to determine how to get rid of him. When he heard of this, Jesus withdrew from the area. Many people followed him and he cured all who had need of it, forcefully commanding them not to disclose their healings.

Jesus' behavior reveals him as the true Servant of Yahweh foretold by Isaiah:

Here is my servant whom I uphold,
my chosen one in whom my soul delights.
I have endowed him with my spirit
that he may bring true justice to the nations.
He does not cry out or shout aloud,
or make his voice heard in the streets.
He does not break the crushed reed,
nor quench the wavering flame.
Faithfully he brings true justice;
He will neither waver, nor be crushed until true justice
is established on earth,
for the islands are awaiting his law. (Is 42:1–4)

The evangelist cites this passage in its entirety because he sees that it is in Jesus that this song of Isaiah is fulfilled. Jesus is the Servant of God, the Chosen, the Beloved in whom the Father delights. He is full of the Spirit, and proclaims everywhere the justice of the kingdom of heaven. He is humble and silent; he neither destroys nor annihilates, but raises up and reestablishes the needy. Therefore, "the islands are awaiting his law."

Jesus Rejoices in the Holy Spirit (Lk 10:21)

Jesus chose seventy-two disciples and sent them two by two to the cities and places where he was going.

The seventy-two returned and said to him, "Lord ... even the devils submit to us when we use your name" (10:17). Jesus replied:

> I watched Satan fall like lightning from heaven. Yes, I have given you power to tread underfoot serpents and scorpions and the whole strength of the enemy; nothing shall ever hurt you. Yet do not rejoice that the spirits submit to you; rejoice rather that your names are written in heaven. (10:18–20)

And Luke comments:

> It was then that, filled with joy by the Holy Spirit he said, "I bless you, Father, Lord of heaven and of earth, for hiding these things from the learned and the clever and revealing them to mere children. Yes, Father, for that is what it pleased you to do. Everything has been entrusted to me by my Father; and no one knows who the Son is except the Father, and who the Father is except the Son and those to whom the Son chooses to reveal him. (10:21–22)

The Holy Spirit, who filled Jesus and was continually leading him, enables him to perceive the victory of God over the kingdom of Satan. Jesus invites his seventy-two disciples to rejoice, not so much because the spirits are subject to them, but because their names are written in heaven.

Jesus exults in a joy that is inspired by the Spirit. He was full of the joy of the Spirit, and at the prompting of the Spirit he breaks forth into prayer. He glorifies his Father, the Lord of heaven and earth, for his plan of salvation. This plan is hidden from the wise and clever, but revealed to the small and humble.

"How much more will the heavenly Father give the Holy Spirit to those who ask him!" (Lk 11:12)

The Gospel passage on the effectiveness of prayer has three sections. The first is an invitation to petitionary prayer and is itself expressed in three parallel phrases:

> Ask, and it will be given to you; search, and you will find; knock, and the door will be opened to you. (11:9)

The second section gives the principle on which the above invitation is based:

> For the one who asks always receives; the one who searches always finds; the one who knocks will always have the door opened to him. (11:10)

The third section is more extensive. It is a parable that draws an even more convincing analogy, serving to make evident and reinforce the truth of the principles just mentioned:

> What father among you would hand his son a stone when he asked for bread? Or hand him a snake instead of a fish? Or hand him a scorpion if he asked for an egg? If you then, who are evil, know how to give your children what is good, how much more will the heavenly Father give the Holy Spirit to those who ask him! (11:11–13)

Matthew has a different rendering of the last part of this passage:

If you, then, who are evil, know how to give your children what is good, how much more will your Father in heaven give good things to those who ask him! (Mt 7:11)

Perhaps the words of Jesus originally ended as recorded in Matthew. If so, Luke may have felt that this ending was too general and decided to retouch it with an explicit mention of the Holy Spirit. Luke has enriched this saying with a deeper spiritual significance: One should ask God for the Holy Spirit, not just for material goods. The Holy Spirit enables us to live according to God's will and so arrive at his kingdom. Luke proclaims that the Holy Spirit is the "good thing," the gift par excellence given by the Father in heaven.

"If it is through the Spirit of God that I cast devils out . . ." (Mt 12:28; Lk 11:20)

Jesus healed a man who was dumb and blind, and possessed by an evil spirit. The astonished onlookers asked, "Can this be the Son of David?" (Mt 12:23b). But upon hearing this the Pharisees said, "This man casts out devils only through Beelzebul, the prince of devils" (12:24). Jesus knew their thoughts and replied:

Every kingdom divided against itself is heading for ruin; and no town, no household divided against itself can stand. Now if Satan casts out Satan, he is divided against himself; so how can his kingdom stand? And if it is through Beelzebul that I cast out devils, through whom do your own experts cast them out? Let them be your judges, then. But if it is through the Spirit of God that I cast devils out, then know that the kingdom of God has overtaken you. (12:25b–28)

This passage is also found in Luke, but with a slight variation at the end: "But if it is through the finger of God that I cast out devils, then know that the kingdom of God has overtaken you" (Lk 11:20).

In Matthew the idea is the same as in Luke. The two expressions "finger of God" and "Spirit of God" both denote the power of God. These passages inspired one of the names used for the Holy Spirit: "The finger at the right hand of the Father."

The text in Luke is an echo of Ex 8:15. In the face of the evidence of the plagues sent upon Egypt by Yahweh, Pharaoh's magicians are forced to confess to their master that "This is the finger of God." Jesus also casts out demons by the finger of God, thanks to the divine power that has been given him.

Matthew's version is even richer. Jesus has received the fullness of the Spirit of God (Mt 3:16) and it is by virtue of the Spirit of God that he casts out demons. This is a sign that the reign of Satan is near its end. The reign of God follows the reign of Satan and with it comes the destruction of all evil (Lk 10:18ff; Jn 12:31ff).

Blasphemy Against the Holy Spirit (Mt 12:31–32; Mk 3:28–30; Lk 12:10)

> And so I tell you, every one of men's sins and blasphemies will be forgiven, but blasphemy against the Spirit will not be forgiven. And anyone who says a word against the Son of Man will be forgiven; but let anyone speak against the Holy Spirit and he will not be forgiven either in this world or in the next. (Mt 12:31–32)

How should one understand this hard saying? This word was Jesus' reaction not only to the incredulity of the Pharisees, but to their perversity in attributing to satanic influence the works he did by the power of the Spirit. Mark writes:

> "But let anyone blaspheme against the Holy Spirit and he will never have forgiveness: he is guilty of an eternal sin." This was because they were saying, "An unclean spirit is in him." (Mk 3:29–30)

When a man refuses to recognize the action of the Holy Spirit, source of pardon and of grace—or worse, when he attributes the works of the Spirit of God to Satan—how can he be forgiven his sin, since he is closing himself off from the source of pardon?

Man may have an excuse for not accepting Jesus, owing to the humble appearances which hide the mystery of the Son of Man, but he cannot be pardoned if he closes his eyes and heart to the wonderful works of the Spirit (see Heb 6:4–6; 10:26–31). E. Boismard, in his work *Synopsis of the Four Gospels*, comments:

> This saying contrasts the sin against the Spirit—the one unforgivable sin—with all other manner of sin or blasphemy, which can be forgiven. The unforgivable gravity of the fault does not come from any supposed superiority of the Spirit of God, or from greater worthiness; rather, it comes from the fact that, by attributing the activity of Jesus to a demonic influence, man refuses to admit that the kingdom of God has arrived, and so places himself outside of that kingdom or rejects it. The "sin" or "blasphemy" is not so much an offense against the Spirit as it is a rejection of the salvation offered by God to man through the Spirit which works in Jesus.*

This word of Jesus is not a condemnation; it is a warning, given so that his listeners may avoid judgment. The passive construction "will never have forgiveness" clearly affirms that forgiveness can come only from God.

The Holy Spirit Prophesies of Jesus in Scripture
(Mt 22:41–46; Mk 12:35–37; Lk 20:41–44)

The episode in which Jesus speaks about David's prophecy in Ps 110 has been preserved in the triple synoptic tradition (Mk 12:35–37; Mt 22:41–46; Lk 20:41–44). Although the accounts of Mark and Luke are similar, their theological goals are slightly different. The Marcan text reads as follows:

---

*Pierre Benoît and M. Emile Boismard, *Synopse des quatre Evangiles, vol. II (Paris: Les Editions du Cerf, 1972), p. 174.

Later, while teaching in the Temple, Jesus said, "How can the scribes maintain that the Christ is the son of David? David himself, moved by the Holy Spirit, said: 'The Lord said to my Lord: Sit at my right hand and I will put your enemies under your feet.' David himself calls him Lord, in what way then can he be his son?" And the great majority of the people heard this with delight. (12:35–37)

Jesus wanted to criticize the teaching of the scribes, men incapable of penetrating the true meaning of scripture because they refused to understand who Jesus really was.

Basing itself on Nathan's prophecy to David in 2 Sm 7:11b–16, Jewish tradition unanimously agreed that the messianic king would be a descendant of David (see also Is 9:5–6; 11:1ff; Jer 23:5; 30:9; 33:15–17; Ex 34:23–24; 37:24; Hos 3:5; Am 9:11; Mi 5:1ff).

But, if the messianic king was to be a descendant, that is, a "son" of David (see Mt 21:9, 15; Mk 10:47), how, then, could David call him "my Lord" in Ps 110:1, a psalm that both the Masoretic tradition and the Septuagint explicitly attribute to David?

In Jewish usage the title of "Lord" was given only in certain relationships: to a Lord by his servants (see Gn 24:12), to a king by his subjects (see Gn 40:1), and to God by his creatures (see Ps 8:2). What then shall we make of the fact that King David could call one of his descendants "my Lord"? Understanding this requires an insight that the scribes do not have, namely, that the messianic king would be much more than an ordinary king. Doesn't Ps 110 place him at the right hand of God, seated at his side to rule the world? The dignity and position of the messianic king means that he transcends all other kings of the earth. It also shows that his kingdom is not of earth, but of heaven. The scribes refuse to understand this; therefore, how would they be able to explain the title of "my Lord" which David gives to his future son?*

Ibid., p. 354.

Here is Matthew's account of the same encounter:

> While the Pharisees were gathered round, Jesus put to them this question, "What is your opinion about the Christ? Whose son is he?" "David's," they told him. "Then how is it" he said "that David, moved by the Spirit, calls him Lord, where he says: 'The Lord said to my Lord: Sit at my right hand and I will put your enemies under your feet'? If David can call him Lord, then how can he be his son?" Not one could think of anything to say in reply, and from that day no one dared to ask him any further questions. (22:41–46a)

As we see, Jesus takes the initiative. In answering his first question the Pharisees see themselves obligated to say that the Messiah is the son of David. Jesus then raises a serious objection: "If David can call him Lord, then how can he be his son?" The evangelist's commentary, "no one dared to ask him any further questions," puts into relief the theological interest and the consequences of any answer.

When Jesus asks the Pharisees their opinion as to whose son the Messiah is, there is a hidden allusion to Ps 2:7b. In this passage God says to his Messiah, "You are my son, today I have become your father."

The Pharisees saw in Jesus only a man, and even if they could have seen in him the messianic king they would not have been able to understand how David could call him "Lord." According to Ps 2:7, however, the Messiah should be the son of God; it is from this relationship that his preeminent dignity springs. Thus is explained why David could give him the title of "Lord."*

For a Christian, both the question and the answer to the question asked by Jesus are clear. Jesus the Messiah was born of David's lineage according to the flesh (Rom 1:3) and is also the Son of God. Therefore, he can be son and Lord of David at the same time.

Mark, as well as Matthew, introduces the quotation from Ps 110:1, saying that King David spoke out of the inspiration of the

---
Ibid.

Holy Spirit. The Holy Spirit was the one who spoke through the prophets, announcing the Messiah as Son of God and son of David; and in the Christian era it is he who continues to reveal the secrets of the mysterious person who is Jesus, the Messiah, the Son of God.

CHAPTER FOUR

THE TEACHING OF JESUS ON THE HOLY SPIRIT

Introduction

Before introducing Jesus in his public ministry, the Gospel of John (like the synoptic gospels) presents Jesus as the Servant of Yahweh. Jesus is the Chosen One of God, the one on whom the Spirit descends to fill him and take possession of him.

> John also declared, "I saw the Spirit coming down on him from heaven like a dove and resting on him. I did not know him myself, but he who sent me to baptize with water had said to me, 'The man on whom you see the Spirit come down and rest is the one who is going to baptize with the Holy Spirit.' Yes, I have seen and I am the witness that he is the Chosen One of God." (Jn 1:32–34)

In this passage there are clear allusions to the great texts of the Book of Isaiah, where reference is made to the Messiah upon whom the spirit of Yahweh rests (11:1ff) and to the Servant of Yahweh, whom he has chosen and in whom he delights (42:1; see 61:1).

Jesus, anointed by the Spirit, will be able to fulfill his messianic mission of baptizing with the Holy Spirit. Only he who has received the fullness of the Spirit can, in turn, give the Spirit to others. But what does it mean, "to baptize with the Holy Spirit"?

Above all, this phrase synthesizes the messianic work of Jesus. To baptize is to wash, to clean, to purify. But the expression "to baptize with the Holy Spirit" means more than this purifying function; there is a higher reality indicated here which can be discovered by going to certain key texts in the Old Testament. The Lord had said through Isaiah:

> I will pour my spirit on your descendants, my blessing on your children. They shall grow like grass where there is plenty of water, like poplars by running streams. (Is 44:3b–4; see also 32:15–17)

Ezekiel had prophesied:

> I shall give you a new heart, and put a new spirit in you; I shall remove the heart of stone from your bodies and give you a heart of flesh instead. I shall put my spirit in you, and make you keep my laws and sincerely respect my observances. You will live in the land which I gave your ancestors. You shall be my people and I will be your God. (Ez 36:26–27)

In these texts the Spirit of God is shown as the source of purification, interior renewal, spiritual fruitfulness, and fidelity to the divine commands. We see in these prophecies that it is by virtue of the Spirit that the definitive covenant of God with his people will be fulfilled.

But it is to the Messiah that the fulfillment of this sublime mission falls (see Is 9:1–6; 11:1–9), and the Messiah is Jesus. The mission of Jesus will be to purify, wash, baptize, and renew men with, in, and through the Spirit. This he accomplishes by the gift and infusion of the divine Spirit.

Just as baptizing in water purifies by pouring or submerging in water, baptizing with the Holy Spirit will purify—and even more, will consecrate— by pouring out or submerging in the Holy Spirit.

Nevertheless, in order for Jesus to baptize with the Holy Spirit it is necessary that he first be lifted up on the cross and then return to his Father. The gift of the Spirit will be poured out from Jesus' glorified body, as if from an inexhaustible fount, upon all humanity (see Jn 7:37–39; 16:7; 19:34; 20:22; Acts 2:33).

Announcement of New Birth Through Water and the Spirit (Jn 3:1–10)

> There was one of the Pharisees called Nicodemus, a leading Jew, who came to Jesus by night and said, "Rabbi, we know that you are a teacher who comes from God; for no one could perform the signs that you do unless God were with him." Jesus answered: "I tell you most solemnly, unless a man is born from above, he cannot see the kingdom of God." (3:1–3)

Nicodemus belonged to the group known as the Pharisees, and was one of the seventy-one members of the Sanhedrin. In addition, he was a "master," well versed in scripture.

He comes to Jesus by night. Nicodemus shows himself open to Jesus' message, since he does come to him; but he comes *at night*, that is to say, his understanding of Jesus is in darkness. He will depend on Jesus, who is the true Light, to illuminate him, and in this way be established in the clear light of day.

Nicodemus addresses Jesus as "Rabbi." On the lips of a Jewish teacher this title signifies a connoisseur and master of the Law and the Prophets.

Jesus responds to Nicodemus in a solemn tone. The expression "I tell you most solemnly" indicates that Jesus is about to make a statement of revelation. Going on to a higher level, he invites Nicodemus to choose all or nothing: to be born again so as to participate in the kingdom of God, or to refuse the new birth and thus be excluded from the kingdom. Jesus answers Nicodemus as if he had asked him how to enter the kingdom (see Mk 10:17–27).

Verse 3 is especially rich in meaning. The expression "Unless a man is born . . ." declares a universal necessity. The verb translated as "born" also has the meaning of "begotten." And an alternate translation of "from above" is "again" (Jn 3:31; 8:23; 11:41; 19:11;

23). The evangelist uses these words in their double meaning. Jesus' intention is to raise the discussion to a higher plane, that is, to deal with a supernatural birth in the sphere of the divine. But Nicodemus (as will be seen by his question) understands the phrase in its earthly sense.

In this context the verb "to see" means "to enter" (see 3:5), "to experience," "to participate in," "to enjoy." John will speak of seeing life (3:36) and seeing death (8:51). Although a very frequent theme in the synoptic gospels, "kingdom of God" appears in John only here and in verse 5, where it means "life," or "eternal life."

> Nicodemus said, "How can a grown man be born? Can he go back into his mother's womb and be born again?" (3:4)

Nicodemus understands Jesus' words on an earthly level, while Jesus moves in the spiritual realm. This incomprehension allows Jesus to develop his thought.

> Jesus replied: "I tell you most solemnly, unless a man is born through water and the Spirit, he cannot enter the kingdom of God." (3:5)

Again the emphatic "I tell you most solemnly" appears, as well as the word "unless," which underlines the absolute necessity of this birth. The expression of verse 3, "born from above" (or "born again"), is now explained as "born [or begotten] through water and the Spirit."

To be begotten obviously implies relation to a father. As a person enters the world because his father begot him, so too, in order for a person to enter the kingdom of heaven he must be begotten by the Father who is in heaven (1 Jn 3:9; 1 Pt 1:23; Ti 3:5).

Eternal life comes to man from God the Father through his Son, to whom he gave the life and power to communicate it (Jn 1:12; 5:21; 26). The idea of divine sonship is found in the Old Testament in connection either with the whole people of Israel (Ex 4:22; Hos 11:1; Dt 32:6) or with the just man (Sir 4:10; 23:1–4; Wis 2:13, 16, 18).

But the text does not say begotten by *God,* but by the *Spirit.* According to biblical tradition, God is the source of life, but even in the creation, life came forth on the earth thanks to the Spirit of God who hovered over the primeval waters (Gn 1:2). Moreover, according to Gn 2:7 the breath is the tangible sign of life; and that breath came to man from the creator, God. Therefore, if man has natural life by virtue of the creative breath of God, eternal life will also be his by the power of the divine Spirit.

It is timely to refer to the Gospel of Luke at this point. God "the Most High" begot Jesus in the womb of Mary through the fruitful action of the Holy Spirit, the Power of the Most High (Lk 1:35). So too, all men, in order to have eternal life and become sons of God, must be begotten by the power of the Spirit. This action of the Spirit is not, therefore, reserved only to some moment in the eschatological future; it refers also to the intimate and fruitful action of the Spirit which communicates eternal life here and now.

The explicit mention of water in Jn 3:5 is an allusion to the sacrament of baptism. Through the action of the Spirit in baptism one enters the kingdom of God, "is born from above," acquires eternal life. The text says, "Unless a man is born through water and the Spirit," alluding first to the water. Therefore, we can suppose that the life-giving action of the Spirit brings about its effect through the baptismal water that bathes the believer. In the letter of Paul to Titus we read: ". . . it was for no reason except his own compassion that he saved us, by means of the cleansing water of rebirth and by renewing us with the Holy Spirit" (Ti 3:5).

> What is born of the flesh is flesh; what is born of the Spirit is spirit. Do not be surprised when I say: You must be born from above. The wind blows wherever it pleases; you hear its sound, but you cannot tell where it comes from or where it is going. That is how it is with all who are born of the Spirit. (Jn 3:6–8)

The noun "flesh" does not have a perjorative sense when used in this context. "Flesh and spirit" do not her designate the two principles of the human make-up, "body and soul," nor the distinction between the material and the spiritual. Rather, "flesh and spirit" express two different situations in which the whole man, the total person, can find himself: Depending upon whether he is situated on the level of human or divine realities, a person may be either "flesh" or "spirit" (see Jn 4:24; 2 Cor 3:17).

Birth according to the flesh is birth into the natural life that all men receive upon coming into the world. Birth according to the Spirit is birth into a life of a superior order, a spiritual or "pneumatic" (from the Greek word *pneuma,* which means "breath" or "spirit") life. Man, in all his human reality, is able to live on two levels, or, to put it differently, can live two lives which are not opposed to each other, but rather which harmonize and complement each other. These are man's natural, "fleshly" life, by virtue of which he is son of his parents, and man's spiritual, "pneumatic" life, by virtue of which he is son of God.

The new birth from above is mysterious but no less real. A comparison with the wind will help make the reality of this spiritual birth clear. The Hebrew word *ruah,* like the Greek word *pneuma,* signifies both wind and spirit. The result is a play on words which communicates a double meaning.

The mystery of the wind intrigued the ancients (for example, see Eccl 11:5). The wind is mysterious and cannot be subdued. It has its own laws, and it "blows wherever it pleases" (Jn 3:7b). One hears its whistling, but does not know whence it comes or to where it goes. Yet we do experience its reality. It is the same with him who is born of the Spirit. His birth is mysterious, solely dependent on the will of the Spirit; nevertheless, this birth is real, and its reality experienced by its fruits (1 Jn 3:10–24).

> "How can that be possible?" asked Nicodemus. "You, a teacher in Israel, and you do not know these things!" replied Jesus. (Jn 3:9–10)

Nicodemus has not understood; he has not been able to rise to the level on which Jesus is speaking. He still remains in the night, symbol of the spiritual darkness in which he came.

In this passage it is not Jesus but Nicodemus who has the title of "teacher." Nonetheless, he is ignorant of all that Jesus is saying. He should at least know from scripture that an outpouring of the

Holy Spirit was prophesied for messianic times (Is 32:15-20; 44:3; Ez 36:26-27; 37:1-14; Jl 3:1-5).

The incomprehension of Nicodemus is absolute and total. The evangelist wants to show us something through this: Knowledge of the things of above is a grace from God and requires an inner change inspired by the Spirit.

After verse 10 Nicodemus disappears from the scene and the dialogue turns into monologue. A discourse now begins in which Jesus will slowly reveal the saving plan of God (3:11-21).

Jesus, Filled with the Spirit, Speaks the Words of God (Jn 3:34)

Jesus is the son of man who has come from above—from heaven. For this reason he is superior to all (3:31). Because he comes from above he can give testimony of the things that he has seen and heard there. But no one accepts his testimony (3:32).

John is of earth and speaks of the things of earth; yet he has accepted the testimony of Jesus. As a result, he has certified and confirmed that God is truthful (3:33).

> He whom God has sent speaks God's own words: God gives him the Spirit without reserve. (3:34)

Jesus can speak of the things of God and the realities of heaven because he is a messenger of God, and God has given him his Spirit without measure. The context of this passage points to the fullness of the messianic Spirit which Jesus received at his baptism (1:32-33).

> The Father loves the Son and has entrusted everything to him. (3:35)

The Father has already given the fullness of his Spirit to the Son. The evangelist will go on to explain little by little all the things the Father has put into the hands of Jesus as a gift (13:3).

The Spirit, Fountain of Life Springing up to Eternal Life (Jn 4:6b–15)

> Jesus, tired by the journey, sat straight down by the well. It was about the sixth hour. When a Samaritan woman came to draw water, Jesus said to her, "Give me a drink." (4:6–7)

Jesus finds himself alone beside the well of Sychar. "His disciples had gone into the town to buy food" (4:8). It was near the sixth hour, that is, noon. This note not only indicates the time, as John frequently does in his Gospel, but also has a deeper meaning: The sun is at its zenith, the time when it is shining in all its splendor; this signifies spiritually that the fullness of the messianic age has arrived.

The meeting at a well of a tired traveler and the woman who come to draw water there is a classic theme in patriarchal literature (Gn 24:10ff; 29:1ff; Ex 2:15–22). In the bible there is a series of poetic stories about wells or springs which has its culmination in this gospel scene (see Gn 2:10ff; 26:15–22; Ex 15:22–27; 17:1–7).

> The Samaritan woman said to him, "What? You are a Jew and you ask me, a Samaritan, for a drink?"—Jews, in fact, do not associate with Samaritans. (4:9)

The woman is surprised that this Jewish man should dare to speak to her and ask her for a drink. The hatred between Jews and Samaritans was traditional (2 Kgs 17:24–41; Ezr 4:3; Lk 9:52–6; Jn 8:48). If the Samaritan woman agreed to give Jesus water to assuage his thrist the evangelist does not tell us, for there is something else that interests him.

Jesus does not respond directly to the woman's question, but speaks to her enigmatically, situating himself on a higher level:

> Jesus replied: "If you only knew what God is offering and who it is that is saying to you: Give me a drink, you would have been the one to ask, and he would have given you living water." (4:10)

"If you knew..." Two things escape the understanding of the woman: recognition of the gift of God, and the identity of the person with whom she is speaking. If the woman had understood these things it would have been she who had asked, and he would have given her living water. The literal meaning of "living water" is "spring water," as opposed to the water of reservoirs and cisterns.

> "You have no bucket, sir," she answered "and the well is deep: how could you get this living water? Are you a greater man than our father Jacob who gave us this well and drank from it himself with his sons and his cattle?" (4:11–12)

This is a typical example of Johannine dialogue in which the characters move on different planes. Jesus spoke on a spiritual level, and the woman remains within the material perspective.

The Samaritan woman addresses Jesus as "sir," a title which she will continue to use with more and more respect (4:15, 19). The woman sees that Jesus has nothing with which to draw water and that the well is deep. If, in spite of that, he still wishes to give her living water from a spring, it must have an unknown origin. Thus her question: "How could you get this living water?" The article "this" shows that it is a specific "living water" that is here at issue. The mysterious origin of Jesus is a very common theme in the Gospel of John (1:38; 2:9; 3:8; 7:27; 13:36; 16:5; 19:9).

With delicate irony the woman asks Jesus, "Are you a greater man that our father Jacob...?" She does not even consider the possibility that Jesus might in fact really be greater than this Patriarch (see 8:53). Her question provokes a more profound response from Jesus.

> Jesus replied: "Whoever drinks this water will get thirsty again; but anyone who drinks the water that I shall give will never be thirsty again: the water that I shall give will turn into a spring inside him, welling up to eternal life." (4:13–14)

Jesus remains on his higher level and continues the revelation step by step. If the water Jesus promises is mysterious in origin

(4:10), it is mysterious also in its nature. Water from a natural source satisfies thirst only for a while. By contrast, the water Jesus promises to give in the future will satisfy thirst forever; what is more, it will become a spring, "welling up to eternal life," within him who drinks of it. A word from the Old Testament provides a background for Jesus' assertion: "You shall be like a watered garden, like a spring of water whose waters never run dry" (Is 58:11; see also Ps 36:9–10).

"Sir," said the woman, "give me some of that water, so that I may never get thirsty and never have to come here again to draw water." (4:15).

Jesus has succeeded in one of his purposes (see 4:10): The woman finally asks him for the living water. But she remains on the level of material realities. She understands that Jesus is offering her a kind of special water, but thinks of it as satiating merely natural thirst. She does not suspect other gifts of a different order and quality. In the face of this offer of living water she remains on the same plane as was Nicodemus when he was confronted with the necessity of new birth.

The living water is presented as a mysterious water through various motifs: 1) it is the gift of God; 2) it comes from Jesus; 3) it satisfies thirst forever; 4) it becomes a fountain springing up to eternal life in him who drinks it.

What spiritual reality is symbolized by the living water? In the Old Testament, spring water is a symbol of a) wisdom and the Law, which are fountains of life (Prv 13:14; Sir 15:1–3; 24:23–34), and b) the life that God will give in the messianic age (Is 12:3; 55:1; Jer 2:13; 17:13; Ez 47:1; etc.).

Using these ideas as a point of departure, some scholars conclude that Jesus was referring to the gift of new life that the incarnate Word had come to bring to the world. This new life is considered under a new aspect: as a gift of God that becomes ours only by a free act of divine generosity.* Fr. Lagrange speaks in

---

*François-Marie Braun, *Evangile selon saint Jean*, in *La Bible Pirot-Clamer* (Paris: Letouzey et Ané, 1950), p. 343.

more scholarly terms: "This gift is clearly what the church calls sanctifying grace, which 1 Jn 3:9 designates by another metaphor, that of the seed of God which remains in him who had been born of God, a seed that is already eternal life (1 Jn 5:11)."*

In the mind of the fourth evangelist the reality symbolized by the living water appears to be the Holy Spirit. Up to this point the central theme of the Gospel has been the installation of the messianic age, and in this the Spirit has had a primary role. Moreover, the Spirit has been presented in conjunction with water, an element charged with symbolism: Jesus is baptized in water, and the Spirit has rested upon him (1:32–33). Jesus comes to purify and to wash, and, in baptizing, to give the Holy Spirit (1:33). The new birth is with water, but this water symbolizes the Spirit, the worker of the mystery (3:5, 8).

A key text that identifies water with the Spirit is Jn 7:37b–39:

"If any man is thirsty, let him come to me! Let the man come and drink who believes in me." As scripture says: From his breast shall flow fountains of living water. He was speaking of the Spirit which those who believed in him were to receive; for there was no Spirit as yet because Jesus had not yet been glorified.

According to this text the living water is the Spirit. To come to Jesus is to believe in him, and the gift of the Spirit follows upon Jesus' glorification. The Holy Spirit springs forth from Jesus to the believer and communicates divine life in such abundance that it is like a "fountain springing up to eternal life" in the heart of the believer (4:14).

The Spirit, Source of the New Worship (Jn 4:23–24)

The dialogue of Jesus and the Samaritan woman changes to a discourse beginning with verse 21. These solemn and majestic verses are the heart and culmination of the conversation of Jesus

---

*Marie-Joseph Lagrange, *Evangile selon saint Jean* (Paris: J. Gabalda, 1948), p. 108.

with the woman of Samaria. The theme is the true worship of the Father.

> Jesus said: "Believe me, woman, the hour is coming when you will worship the Father neither on this mountain nor in Jerusalem. You worship what you do not know; we worship what we do know; for salvation comes from the Jews. But the hour will come—in fact it is here already—when true worshipers will worship the Father in spirit and truth: that is the kind of worshiper the Father wants." (4:21-24)

"Believe me, woman . . ." Jesus is going to say something that is beyond the scope of the woman's ability to understand on a natural, human level. Therefore, he requires of her an act of faith, of total surrender.

"The hour is coming," that is, a moment established by God is coming in which worship will transcend places and races. Both Jerusalem and Gerizim belong to the things of earth. The object of worship is God the Father. This is the first time in the Fourth Gospel that the title of "Father" is given to God in his dealings with men.

Verse 22 changes the focus and is a qualification in favor of the Jews. "Salvation comes from the Jews." No word of higher praise has been written concerning the privileges of Israel (see Rom 3:1-2; 9:4-5). The term "salvation" is used to translate the Greek word *soteria* and the Hebrew *yeshuah*. A play on words in Aramaic gives a particular vigor to the idea and uncovers a wealth of meaning. *Yeshuah* is very similar to *Yeshua*, the Hebrew word for "Jesus." Thus verse 22 can be explained as follows: By the eternal consent of God, the perfect salvation which is Jesus has sprung forth from the Jewish people.

Verse 23 continues the thought of verse 21. The eschatological future is clarified by the temporal expression, "is here already." This is already the moment.

In the phrase "when true worshipers . . ." the adjective "true" means "authentic." The Father will only be truly—or authentically—worshiped if his worshipers do it "in spirit and truth."

In spirit. This apparently concerns interior worship, as opposed to purely exterior worship consisting of rites and ceremonies which lack soul and spirit. Such an understanding of "in spirit" was already being expressed by the ancient prophets (Am 5:21–25; Is 1:11ff; Jer 6:20; Ps 50:7–23). From the perspective of the Fourth Gospel, however, the expression should mean much more.

For John, the Spirit is the one who, in coming down and resting upon Jesus, begins the messianic age (1:32ff). It is the Spirit who purifies in the messianic baptism (1:33) and who works the new birth (3:5–8). The Spirit will also be the founder of a new kind of worship, one that is proper to messianic times (see Rom 8:26–27).

And truth. This expression, together with the preceeding modifier, "true," very likely means that the worship of the Father which is founded by the Spirit will be genuinely authentic worship.

If one draws out the implications of the possible Semitic origin of the text, the tone would be different: We would have here an idea parallel to Jn 1:14 (faithfulness, firmness, and permanence). Thus the worship of the Father in spirit and truth would be a worship which, born by the impulse of the Spirit, is authentically interior, supernatural, and divine, and, consequently, firm, faithful, stable, and permanent.

It is even possible that the word "truth" means Jesus himself. In the first place, according to 1:51 and 2:21 Jesus will be the new house of God, the new altar, the new Temple where the presence of God is found. Besides, for the evangelist Jesus is the Truth (14:6), since he reveals the truth of God to men (8:45; 18:37). The Spirit, who has filled Jesus, is the Spirit of truth who leads to the whole truth (14:17; 15:26; 16:13–15). This being so, true worshipers who seek the Father are those who, moved by the Spirit, adore the Father through Jesus.

This interpretation is illustrated by Jesus' reply to Philip's question, "Lord, let us see the Father and we shall be satisfied." Jesus answered:

> Have I been with you all this time, Philip, and you still do not know me? To have seen me is to have seen the Father, so how can you say, "Let us see the Father"? Do you not believe that I am in the Father and the Father is in me? (14:8–10a)

In the Old Testament "spirit" ordinarily refers not so much to a mode of being which is opposed to matter, but rather to a principle of life, a creative activity. Applied to God, "spirit" means a higher principle of life, transcending all creatures. In other words, "God is Spirit" means that God belongs to a higher sphere, properly his own.

In John's Gospel "spirit" has this same meaning. Therefore, to worship the Father it is necessary to be raised up by a source of spiritual life which is at God's level. The revelation of God can have God alone as its source (1:18); birth to a life from above can only come from God (3:6). This is also true for authentic worship of the Father.

The Samaritan woman receives this revelation without comprehending it. Not understanding, and as one who wishes to end the conversation, she says:

> I know that Messiah—that is, Christ—is coming; and when he comes he will tell us everything. (4:25)

At this time the Samaritans were waiting for a Messiah whose name would be Taheb, which means "he who returns" or "he who restores." More than a military commander, he was to be a prophet like Moses (Dt 18:15) who would have a religious mission as lawgiver and revealer. The role of revealer is alluded to by the Samaritan when she says, "he will tell us everything." Taheb would reunite Jews and Gentiles and gloriously govern over all.

> "I who am speaking to you," said Jesus, "I am he." (4:26)

Jesus ends the dialogue by openly and clearly proclaiming his messiahship. He is the one who is awaited. He is not coming in the future—he is already present. He is the one who had been sent by God to "tell us everything." His messianic mission is a mission of revelation. Jesus, the Word of God, speaks naturally of the things of God. Jesus identifies himself with the Taheb of Samaritan expectations. Declaring himself the Messiah, he is conscious that in him the words of the prophets are fulfilled. He also knows that he is the Anointed of the Spirit (Is 11:1; 42:1; 61:1) and that he is thus both the revealer of the Father, and the giver of the Spirit in the messianic age.

The Spirit, the Source of Life (Jn 6:63)

> After hearing it, many of his followers said, "This is intolerable language. How could anyone accept it?" Jesus was aware that his followers were complaining about it and said, "Does this upset you? What if you should see the Son of Man ascend to where he was before? It is the spirit that gives life, the flesh has nothing to offer. The words I have spoken to you are spirit and they are life. But there are some of you who do not believe... This is why I told you that no one could come to me unless the Father allows him." (6:60–65)

An opposition between spirit and flesh is presented here. It is the same contrast that appeared earlier in 3:6. Jesus speaks of two principles:

The *flesh* is the natural principle found on the plane of earthly realities. This principle, without being bad in itself, is powerless to know and work the things of God (see Mt 16:17).

The *spirit* is the principle found on the level of divine realities. The Lord alone is capable of imparting eternal life and making known the things of God (see Jn 3:5; 6, 8; 4:24).

Earlier in the Gospel the Father and the Son were spoken of as giving life (5:21); this ability is now applied to the Spirit. Jesus' ascension to the Father will be necessary, for only in this way will he be able to send his disciples the Spirit of truth. The spirit will give them eternal life and enable them to understand all he has shown them (see 7:38–39; 14:26; 26:7, 12–13; 20:22).

The words of Jesus are *spirit* and *life,* that is, they belong to the sphere of divine, spiritual realities, the things "from above." They are efficacious in themselves, being creative acts which go beyond the limits of human reason. They bring eternal life. Therefore, it is not strange for Jesus' words to one day truly transform bread and wine into his flesh and blood.

"But there are some of you who do not believe." Jesus' supernatural knowledge again comes to the fore. Jesus is the one to whom the Father has given the Spirit without measure. Jesus knew from the beginning who was and who was not going to believe in him, and who was going to betray him. Only those who receive the free gift of faith from the Father can believe in Jesus.

The Promise of the Spirit: Living Water (Jn 7:37–39)

It was the feast of Tabernacles, the most important Jewish feast in the time of Jesus. This feast was associated with the coming of the Day of Yahweh (Zec 9–14). It was also the occasion on which the Lord was entreated to supply the rain that would assure the fertility of the fields.

On each of the seven days of the feast a procession took place from the fountain of Gihon to the Temple. The priest took water from the fountain and carried it in a jug in the procession. The rest of the people carried branches, which symbolized tents, and pieces of fruit, which symbolized the harvest. During the procession they sang the psalms of the Hallel, Ps 113–118. On arriving at the altar of holocausts the priest made a circle around the altar and poured the water on it. On the seventh day, the most solemn day of the feast, everyone walked around the altar seven times.

This year on the last, the greatest day of the festival, Jesus stood up and cried out, saying:

> If any man is thirsty, let him come to me! Let the man come and drink who believes in me! As Scripture says: From his breast shall flow fountains of living water. (7:37–38)

This word of Jesus is punctuated differently from manuscript to manuscript. The interpretation of the passage will depend upon which punctuation is preferred. There are two principal possibilities, the translation given above and the one that follows:

> If any man is thirsty, let him come to me and drink. He who believes in me, as scripture says, from his breast shall flow fountains of living water.

The second text is supported by papyri #66 and #75; by Fathers of the church such as Athanasius, Cyril of Jerusalem, and Basil, (and also by Origen); and by modern commentators such as Wescott, Schlatter, Bernard, Lightfoot, Bover, Dubarle, and others.

The meaning of this text is not difficult to determine. Whoever would quench his thirst, let him go to Jesus and drink. The water he receives will become so abundant in him that from his breast will spring forth rivers of living water. Thus the believer is the source of living water. The best commentary on this text is given earlier by the evangelist in the dialogue of Jesus and the Samaritan woman (4:13–14).

The most likely source of the scripture passage to which Jesus refers is Is 58:10b–11.

> Yahweh will always guide you.... And you shall be like a watered garden, like a spring of water whose waters never run dry.

Other possible references are Zec 14:8; Prv 4:23; 5:15; 18:4; Sir 24:30–33.

The first text is supported by Latin manuscripts of the second century; by Fathers of the church such as Irenaeus, Cyprian, and Hippolytus; and by modern commentators such as Loisy, Bultmann, Barrett, Jeremias, Dodd, Braun, Boismard, Brown, Mollat, and others.

A christological interpretation is what results from this punctuation. Jesus is again presented as the giver of living water (see 4:10; 19:34; 20:22; Rv 22:1). Whoever is thirsty and believes in Jesus, let him go to Jesus and drink, for scripture says that rivers of living water will flow from Jesus' breast.

In this case the scripture reference would not be a quotation from a definite text. The passages that refer to the rock from which water came forth in the desert are possible allusions (Ex 17:5–6; Nm 20:7–11; Ps 78:15–16, 24; 104:8; 105:40ff; Dt 8:15; Is 43:20; 44:3; 48:21; see also 1 Cor 10:4). Also possible are those texts which refer to the river of water that goes out from the new Temple, as described in Ez 47:1–11 and mentioned in Zec 14:8 (see also Jn 2:21; Rv 22:1ff).

Which of the two punctuations is to be preferred? Perhaps the first, since the christological interpretation that follows from it harmonizes perfectly with the significance of the feast of Tabernacles. In Jn 7:37–38 Jesus offers himself as the authentic source of living water. His body is the new Temple (2:21) and is the spring from which will run rivers of living water. Only one condition is necessary for receiving this water: going to Jesus and believing in him.

To what reality does Jesus refer when he employs the symbol of living water? The evangelist reveals it as follows:

> He was speaking of the Spirit which those who believed in him were to receive; for there was no Spirit as yet because Jesus had not yet been glorified. (7:39)

Ancient versions and some of the Fathers gave a somewhat different rendering of the phrase "there was no Spirit as yet." That rendering is, "the Spirit had not yet been given." However, since this second version is concerned more with God in his relations with men than with the mystery of God in himself, the first text is to be preferred.

We see, therefore, that in the plan of salvation the total, abundant, messianic outpouring of the Spirit was conditional upon the glorification of Jesus through his death, resurrection, and ascension (16:7; 19:30, 34; 20:22; Acts 2:33). The Spirit is the living water, the gift of God springing forth from the glorified Jesus, whom Jesus gives to whoever believes in him.

The Promise of Another Paraclete, the Spirit of Truth (Jn 14:15–17)

> If you love me you will keep my commandments. I shall ask the Father, and he will give you another Advocate to be with you forever, that Spirit of truth whom the world can never receive since it neither sees nor knows him; but you know him, because he is with you, he is in you. (14:15–17)

The themes of love and of observance of the commandments form the context within which the promise of another Advocate (or Paraclete) is found (14:15, 21, 23, 24). The proof of true, authentic love for Jesus is the keeping of his commandments. Observing them assures staying in his love. In his relationship with his Father, Jesus is the greatest example of love and observance of the Father's precepts (15:10).

It is not enough to know the commandments; it is necessary to keep them. Whoever does this truly loves Jesus (14:21; 1 Jn 5:3; 2 Jn 6). Contrapositively, whoever does not observe the commandments of Jesus does not love him (14:24).

The ultimate source of Jesus' teaching is his Father who sent him (14:24). Therefore, the commandments and words of Jesus are the commandments and words of the Father. Whoever keeps them will be the object of the Father's love (14:21, 23).

The greatest fruit of obedient love is the gift of another Paraclete. The word "Paraclete" appears in four other passages in John's Gospel (14:26; 15:26–27; 16:7–11, 12–14).

Two principal ideas are expressed in 14:16a: The Paraclete is a gift of the Father to the disciples, won by the supplication of Jesus; and he is "another" Paraclete, in contrast to a "first" Paraclete.

John usually applies the title of "Paraclete" to the Holy Spirit. But in 1 Jn 2:1 the author uses this same title to refer to Jesus. If this name is given to Jesus as well as to the Spirit, it must have a significance applicable to both. The Greek word *parakletos* is derived from *para-kaleo,* which means "to call so as to be at the side of." Jesus, as well as the Spirit, has fulfilled this mission, although in a different way.

Jesus is the Son of God. He is the one sent by the Father to be with men. Even more, "God loved the world so much that he gave his only Son, so that everyone who believes in him may not be lost but may have eternal life" (3:14–15). To sum up, Jesus is the Son, the one who is sent, the gift of the Father to men. He is the *Parakletos,* that is, the one called to be at our side.

The Holy Spirit, in Jesus' own words, is another Paraclete, another one called to be at the side of men. Like Jesus, the Spirit is another gift of the Father (14:16) and another one who is sent (14:26). And he is this thanks to the intercession of Jesus.

What is the mission of this other Paraclete, this "sent one," this gift of the Father? The answer is at once simple and profound.

In the Bible a name is viewed as something very significant. It is actually a description of one's personal mission. Therefore, the mission of the second Paraclete is the same as that of the first Paraclete. We can see this from the context of the passage. Jesus is about to leave the world and return to his Father. He is going to leave his disciples, but he will not leave them alone: "I shall ask the Father, and he will give you another Advocate to be with you forever" (14:16). This new Advocate or Paraclete, will fulfill the same mission as Jesus by being with his disciples. Not having a human nature with a corruptible body, he will not be subject to the laws of death. He will not disappear, but will remain forever.

It is obvious, however, that the Holy Spirit did not carry out a mission identical to that carried out by Jesus. Clearly, for example, he did not give up his life on the cross. What mission, then, does the Spirit have in common with the first Paraclete? The answer is found in 14:17, where Jesus speaks of the Advocate as:

> That Spirit of truth whom the world can never receive since it neither sees nor knows him; but you know him, because he is with you, he is in you.

"Spirit of truth" is an expression charged with meaning. A little earlier in the account (14:6) Jesus had defined himself as the Truth, thus summing up all his work of revelation. He has spoken the truth that he heard from his Father (8:40, 45), truth which enlightens, gives life, sets free (8:12, 32), truth which excludes all sin (8:46), truth which is radically opposed to the evil one, deception, and death (8:40). The Spirit, remaining with the disciples, will continue in and among the disciples the revelatory work of Jesus, who is the Truth. For that reason the Spirit is called the Spirit of truth.

Just as the world did not receive Jesus, nor recognize him as the one sent by the Father, neither will the world receive or know or see the Spirit. On the other hand, since the disciples received and knew Jesus (14:7b–11) they will also know the Spirit, who will dwell with them and be in them (14:17b).

The Spirit, the other Paraclete, is the gift given by the Father. He will remain forever with and in the disciples, carrying out the same revelatory work of Jesus, who is the Truth. As R. Brown says: "The Paraclete/Spirit will differ from Jesus the Paraclete in that the Spirit is not corporeally visible and his presence will only be by indwelling in the disciples."*

The future "will give" (14:16) and the present "is with.... is in" (14:17) complement, rather than contradict, one another. "Will give" is looking forward to the glorification of Jesus (7:39), and "is with... is in" supposes a fulfilled eschatology. We should remember that the Gospel was written when the glorification of Jesus and the gift of the Spirit had already taken place.

The Paraclete, the Holy Spirit who Teaches and Reminds (Jn 14:25–26)

> I have said these things to you while still with you; but the Advocate, the Holy Spirit, whom the Father will send in my name, will teach you everything and remind you of all I have said to you. (14:25–26)

The Paraclete, the Spirit of truth, here receives a third title: the "Holy Spirit." In the Old Testament, holiness is an essentially divine attribute. And in the Fourth Gospel the adjective "holy" is applied to Jesus ("Holy One of God" [6:69]), the Father (17:11), and especially the Holy Spirit (1:33; 7:39; 14:26; 20:22).

The expression "whom the Father will send in my name" has profound meaning: It points to the close bonds of unity between Jesus and the Spirit, like the union which exists between Jesus and the Father (see 16:13–15; 17:11–12).

The Holy Spirit has received a double mission from the Master: 1) to teach the disciples all things, and 2) remind the disciples of what Jesus said.

---

*Raymond E. Brown, *The Gospel According to John,* in *The Anchor Bible* (Garden City, N.Y.: Doubleday, 1970), p. 644.

1. Jesus received from the Father the charge of teaching, and all that he heard from his Father he communicated to his disciples:

> I shall not call you servants any more, because a servant does not know his master's business; I call you friends, because I have made known to you everything I have learned from my Father. (15:15; see also 8:28–29)

It is now the Holy Spirit who is the teacher and who continues that mission of Jesus.

The phrase "will teach you everything" could mean that the Spirit is going to give the disciples a complete knowledge of all that is. There is a better interpretation, however, namely, that the Holy Spirit (as Jesus before him) will teach the disciples all that the Father would want them to know of his plan of salvation (16:13–15). In this respect the Holy Spirit takes the place of Jesus, and will communicate to the future community whatever teachings may be necessary later on.

2. The promise to remind the disciples of what Jesus said will consist not only of bringing to mind the things of the past, but of opening up the profound meaning of Jesus' works and words (2:17, 22; 12:16). The evangelist himself has written his book by the light of the Spirit and, therefore, has contemplated the works of Jesus as signs of spiritual realities.

But the Paraclete, the Spirit of truth which is the Holy Spirit, has been given by the Father, at the request of Jesus, that he might be at the side of the disciples forever (14:15). This being so, the mission of the Spirit will continue in the Christian community through all centuries. His mission will always be a mission of truth and of teaching, based on the works and words of Jesus. His revealing action will draw out the profound meaning of those "signs" in order to enlighten every epoch of history.

The Testimony of the Paraclete (Jn 15:26–27)

> When the Advocate comes, whom I shall send to you from the Father, the Spirit of truth who issues from the Father, he will

be my witness. And you too will be witnesses, because you have been with me from the outset. (15:26–27)

This text offers us another fact. The Holy Spirit, who comes to us from the Father, will come, sent not only by the Father (14:25), but also by Jesus.

Systematic theology has made use of 15:26 in understanding the sending out of the Spirit in the mystery of God. It has seen in the word "issues" evidence for the eternal emanation or procession of the Spirit from the Father. These distinctions, however, go beyond the primary sense of the text.

The Spirit of truth comes in order to bear witness to Jesus. Jesus addressed the world and bore witness to himself (8:13–14). He proved the truth of his revelation by means of works that no one had ever done. But the world did not believe; it even hated Jesus and his Father, and still hates and persecutes his disciples. With this attitude the world has sunk to the depths of sin.

But will everything end in this gloomy state in which the world has rejected Jesus and his Father, in which evil has apparently triumphed? In no way! The Spirit of truth, the Paraclete, called to be at the side of the disciples and who lives in their hearts (14:17), will bear witness to Jesus. In so doing, he will judge the world. The Spirit's mission of testimony on behalf of Jesus is described more fully in 16:8–11.

The Spirit's witness to Jesus is not isolated; the disciples will also be witnesses. Nevertheless, the testimony of the Spirit and the testimony of the disciples do not constitute two testimonies, but only one. This is consistent with a word of Jesus found in the synoptic Gospels:

And when they lead you away to hand you over, do not worry beforehand about what to say; no, say whatever is given to you when the time comes, because it is not you who will be speaking: it will be the Holy Spirit. (Mk 13:11; see also Mt 10:20; Lk 12:12; Acts 5:32; 15:28)

The disciples, then, are intimately associated with the mission of testimony which the Holy Spirit carries out on behalf of Jesus.

The reason for this is the friendship and brotherhood they have had with Jesus since the beginning. Their experience of living together with him is the source of their knowledge, and this knowledge, or personal understanding, is the basis of their ability to testify. The disciples have heard Jesus and seen him with their own eyes. Therefore, they will be able to bear witness to him (1 Jn 1:2).

It is the same for the Spirit. If the Spirit bears witness to Jesus, it be because he knows him, as indeed he knew him from the beginning, because before Abraham was made, he existed (see Jn 1:1; 8:53; 17:5).

If Jesus Goes, He Will Send the Spirit (Jn 16:4b–7)

> I did not tell you this from the outset, because I was with you; but now I am going to the one who sent me. Not one of you has asked, "Where are you going?" Yet you are sad at heart because I have told you this. Still, I must tell you the truth: it is for your own good that I am going because unless I go, the Advocate will not come to you; but if I do go, I will send him to you. (16:4b–7)

A number of important ideas are expressed in these words. Their significance is emphasized by the phrase "I must tell you the truth." Jesus wishes to reveal something transcendent.

It is to the disciples' advantage that Jesus goes, for if he does not go the Advocate (or Paraclete) cannot come. If Jesus goes he will send the Paraclete. But why is it necessary that the Holy Spirit come to the disciples?

The answer has to do with the mission of bearing witness to Jesus that is assigned to the Spirit of truth (15:26; 16:8–11). The world hated Jesus, persecuted him, and put him to death. Who will come to his defense? Who will take up his cause? Who will work justice? The Paraclete, who will be at the side of the disciples, will do this; and even more, he will dwell in them! (14:17; 15:26–27). But *why* must Jesus go? Is it possible that his presence and the presence of the Paraclete are incompatible?

In the first place, the departure of Jesus is not so much his disappearance as his return to the Father. In the second place, the gift of the Paraclete was conditional, according to the divine plan, upon the glorification of Jesus by his death and resurrection (7:39).

The presence of the glorified Jesus and the presence of the Spirit are not opposed to one another (14:16,23). What is opposed, according to the plan of God, is the presence of the earthly Jesus and the full gift of the Spirit.

The Spirit is like a prize that Jesus wins when he has fulfilled the work the Father has entrusted to him (Jn 19:30, 34).

The Spirit Will Show the World its Unrighteousness (Jn 16:8–11)

> And when he comes, he will show the world how wrong it was, about sin, and about who was in the right, and about judgment: about sin: proved by their refusal to believe in me; about who was in the right: proved by my going to the Father and your seeing me no more; about judgment: proved by the prince of this world being already condemned. (16:8–11)

The Paraclete, who Jesus will send on behalf of the Father, and who will both be at the side of the disciples and dwell in them, will show the world the unrighteousness of its actions in regard to Jesus. In other words, the Holy Spirit will cause it to be seen and understood that in the proceedings against Jesus it was the world which was in error, not Jesus. The disciples will be able to bear witness to Jesus against the world (15:26–27). This role of the Paraclete as accuser of the world and defender of Jesus touches on three areas: sin, justice, and judgment.

"About sin: proved by their refusal to believe in me." The Paraclete will prove that the world is guilty of the basic sin of not believing in Jesus. The evangelist had expressed that rejection in the prologue of the Gospel: "And the world did not know him" (1:10). This theme is emphasized throughout the entire work.

Jesus says to Nicodemus:

On these grounds is sentence pronounced: that though the light has come into the world men have shown they prefer darkness to the light because their deeds were evil. (3:19)

Jesus' own brothers did not believe in him (7:5). At the end of his ministry, "though they had been present when he gave so many signs, they did not believe in him" (12:37). Lack of faith is the ultimate explanation for Jesus betrayal:

"But there are some of you who do not believe." For Jesus knew from the outset those who did not believe, and who it was that would betray him. (6:64)

"About who was in the right: proved by my going to the Father and your seeing me no more." The Paraclete will show who was in the right. Given the context, the expression "who was in the right" means "who has justice on his side." Justice must be here understood in the technical, legal sense, not in its broader meaning and even less in the sense of God's "saving justice" as spoken of in Rom 1:17 and 3:21–22.

The Paraclete will prove that the world was in error when it branded Jesus a transgressor of the Law (5:18), a seducer (7:12), a sinner and demoniac (8:48; 9:24), and a blasphemer, (10:33). It was unjust in condemning him to death. Jesus was right, and justice cries out in his favor.

The proof of this is that Jesus is going to the Father (13:1; 14:12, 28; 16:28; 20:17). His glorification is the strongest argument that he was founded in the truth, that he was speaking the truth (8:40), that he had come to bear witness to the truth (19:37), and that he was the Truth (14:6). Having returned to his Father, Jesus enjoys the divine glory that he possessed as his own since before the creation of the world (17:5).

"Your seeing me no more." This bodily disappearance of Jesus is the necessary consequence of his rising to the Father. Once glorified, Jesus no longer belongs to this world; he escapes the dimensions of the terrestrial condition. Nevertheless, he will come in a mysterious way, together with the Father, to make his dwelling within the disciples. There, within the disciples, the Holy Spirit will bear witness to him (14:17, 23; 15:26).

"About judgement: proved by the prince of this world being already condemned." The prince of this world was certainly going to play an important role in the passion and death of Jesus, and would appear to have gained the victory. Nevertheless, the Spirit will make it known that the prince of this world had no power over Jesus (14:30). As a matter of fact, Jesus freely and voluntarily delivered himself up to death for love of his Father; he freely and voluntarily set himself to carry out the mandate he had received (10:18; 14:31). His exaltation to the same glory as the Father will be in itself the most eloquent proof of his definitive victory over Satan. The words of Jesus on Palm Sunday are the best commentary on verse 11:

> Now sentence is being passed on this world; now the prince of this world is to be overthrown. And when I am lifted up from the earth, I shall draw all men to myself (12:31–32)

The Spirit Will Guide the Disciples into the Truth (Jn 16:12–15)

> I still have many things to say to you but they would be too much for you now. But when the Spirit of truth comes he will lead you to the complete truth, since he will not be speaking as from himself but will say only what he has learned; and he will tell you of the things to come. He will glorify me, since all he tells you will be taken from what is mine. Everything the Father has is mine; that is why I said: All he tells you will be taken from what is mine. (16:12–15)

In this passage Jesus again presents the Spirit as the great teacher of truth (see 14:26).

What things can Jesus still have to say to his disciples, since he himself solemnly declared, "I have made known to you everything I have learned from my Father" (15:15b)? According to John the most appropriate sense in which to understand this statement is the following. There was much more that Jesus could still have told them about his Father, himself, the mission he was fulfilling and had almost completed, and about the deep meaning of all he had said and done during his life. But it would have been useless, for they could not then have understood it. An alternate translation of 16:12b is, "you cannot bear them now." The Greek verb here rendered "bear" concerns weight that is necessary to carry. When Jesus is raised from the dead (2:22) and glorified (12:16) the disciples will be able to understand more deeply his mission and work (see 13:7).

Thanks to the action of the Spirit of truth the disciples will be able to know the profound meaning of all that Jesus said and did during his ministry. This Spirit will guide and lead them and "bring them down the road." The Greek verb translated in 16:13 by "lead" is a derivative of the noun "road" or "way." Referring to himself Jesus said, "I am the Way" (14:6).

The Spirit will bring the disciples down the road of all truth. But what is the truth? Jesus had said, "If you make my work your home you will indeed be my disciples, you will learn the truth and the truth will make you free" (8:31-32). Further on he says, "As it is, you want to kill me when I tell you the truth as I have learned it from God" (8:40). And when Thomas wanted to know the way, Jesus answered, "I am the Way, the Truth and the Life" (14:6).

Once again, the work of the Spirit will be to lead the Apostles in the true way of Jesus the Truth. The Spirit's light will not only uncover for them the theoretical meaning of the words and works of Jesus, but will guide and move them to live in accordance with the master's words and commands (14:15-24).

The evangelist writes in the discourse of Jesus and Nicodemus: "The man who lives by the truth comes out into the light" (3:21). Jesus will say to Pilate: "All who are on the side of truth listen to my voice" (18:37). To hear Jesus is to receive him, and to receive him is to believe in him and keep his commandments.

The Holy Spirit, the Paraclete sent by the Father in the name of Jesus, will always be with the disciples, continuing in them the revelatory mission of Jesus, the Truth (see 1 Jn 2:27). Some texts of the Old Testament may be in the back of John's mind: Ps 143:10

("teach me to obey you . . . may your good spirit guide me on to level ground"); perhaps Is 63:14 and Ps 25:4–6.

The Spirit will be able to carry out this mission of truth "since he will not be speaking as from himself but will say only what he has learned" (16:13). The union which exists between Jesus and the Spirit is like that between Jesus and the Father. And as Jesus spoke only what he heard from his Father, so the Spirit will speak only what he hears from Jesus.

What does it mean, "he will tell you of the things to come"? Is this an allusion to the charism of prophecy of which other New Testament writings speak (e.g. Acts 21:10–14)? Such an interpretation does not seem to fit in with the rest of John's presentation in the Gospel. When the Samaritan woman says, in alluding to the hoped-for Messiah, "when he comes, he will tell us everything," Jesus responds with the revelation of his own self: "I am he, who is speaking to you!" (Jn 4:25). There then follows the wonderful scene of the Samaritans who go out to Jesus and believe in him. In this passage the revelatory role of Jesus is in direct relation to the faith of the Samaritans who believe in him.

Therefore, we are to understand that the revealing action of the Spirit who will announce what is to come consists not in revealing new things, but in uncovering and making understood, through all centuries and in each generation, the deep meaning of the person and mission of Jesus. This is the active, perpetual assistance of the Spirit which Jesus promised to his disciples (14:16). Jesus refers to the teaching and reminding role of the Spirit when he says, "But the Advocate, the Holy Spirit, whom the Father will send in my name, will teach you everything and remind you of all I have said to you" (14:26).

"He will glorify me, since all he tells you will be taken from what is mine." As Jesus glorified his Father on earth, revealing his name to men and bringing to completion the work entrusted to him (17:4, 6), so also the Spirit will glorify Jesus, revealing him and bearing witness to him throughout all time. The Spirit of truth will be able to fulfill that mission because what he says is what he receives from Jesus.

"Everything the Father has is mine; that is why I said: All he tells you will be taken from what is mine." This passage on the

Spirit ends by referring again to the relationship of the Spirit to the Father. The Paraclete, the Spirit of truth, the Holy Spirit, proceeds from the Father, is sent by the Father, and is a gift from the Father (14:16, 26; 15:26).

And because the Father and the Son share everything (17:10) the Spirit of truth is sent also by Jesus, and is a gift of Jesus to men. Later theology will say that the Holy Spirit proceeds from the Father and from the Son as from one source: *Qui a Patre Filioque procedit.*

CHAPTER FIVE

THE GIFT OF THE SPIRIT

According to the divine plan conceived by the Father from all eternity, the messianic gift of the Spirit was conditional upon the glorification of Jesus (7:39; 16:7). For John the mystery of the glorification of Jesus includes three elements: his death, his resurrection, and his ascension (see 20:17).

From this perspective the death of the Son of Man on the cross is already the beginning of his triumph and glorious exaltation.

> The Son of Man must be lifted up as Moses lifted up the serpent in the desert, so that everyone who believes may have eternal life in him. (3:14–15)
>
> When you have lifted up the Son of Man, then you will know that I am He. (8:28a)
>
> Now sentence is being passed on this world; now the prince of this world is to be overthrown. And when I am lifted up from the earth, I shall draw all men to myself. (12:31–32).

With this context established, it is not strange that the evangelist begins to speak, though very discreetly, of the gift of the Spirit right from the majestic moments when Jesus is about to breathe his last on the height of the cross.

"I Am Thirsty!" (Jn 19:28–29)

> After this, Jesus knew that everything had now been completed, and to fulfill the scripture perfectly he said: "I am thirsty." A jar full of vinegar stood there, so putting a sponge soaked in the vinegar on a hyssop stick, they held it up to his mouth. (19:28–29)

This account of Jesus' foreknowledge reveals the emphasis and nuance that John, in particular, gives the event. Jesus knows all with supernatural knowledge. He goes about directing, step by step, the details of his passion-exaltation on the cross. He knows that all is now finished and, therefore, that scripture can now be fulfilled. In view of that he says, "I am thirsty." This statement is full of meaning and is explainable on two levels.

The most obvious meaning derives from the physical circumstances of the event. It is in this line of interpretation that scripture scholars cite Ps 69:21, "When I was thirsty they gave me vinegar to drink," as the text to which Jesus refers. He was thirsty, they gave him vinegar, and thus that which was prophesied in this psalm was fulfilled (see also Jn 19:23ff, 36ff).

The deeper meaning has not been made explicit by the evangelist himself, who records simply that Jesus said "I am thirsty" so that scripture might be fulfilled. What, therefore, is the deeper meaning of "I am thirsty"? Some scripture scholars try to answer this question by citing two texts from psalms where the psalmist expresses his thirst for God (Ps 42:2, 63:1). It is probably necessary, however, to explore a different direction.

Jesus knows that "everything had now been completed," that nothing is lacking. Yet he adds, "I am thirsty" so as to fulfill scripture. Hence it appears that the word of the evangelist—"to fulfill the scripture perfectly"—refers to scripture as a whole, not just to the statement "I am thirsty." The evangelist is referring to all the messianic prophecies or intimations of the divine plan of salvation (e.g. Jer 31:31–34; Ez 11:19–20; 36:26–27; 47:1–12).

Jesus declared himself thirsty on another occasion, when he said to the Samaritan woman "Give me a drink" (4:7). Jesus was thirsty, and so asked for water. But besides natural thirst, Jesus the Messiah was burning with another thirst, a deep thirst to give rather than receive. In the conversation with the Samaritan he added immediately:

> If you only knew what God is offering and who it is that is saying to you: Give me a drink, you would have been the one to ask, and he would have given you living water. (4:10)

And at the end of the dialogue Jesus gets the woman to ask:

> Sir . . . give me some of that water so that I may never get thirsty and never have to come here again to draw water. (4:15)

It is the same situation here on the cross. With his supernatural knowledge Jesus knows that his mission is complete, the work of the Father has been fulfilled, and salvation has been won. The fruits of the life and sacrifice of Jesus can now be poured out on the whole world. Nothing is lacking. Scripture can now be fulfilled, and it is for this that Jesus is thirsty. The outpouring of the Spirit which was announced by the prophets can now come and inaugurate the messianic age in all fullness, and seal the new covenant in the heart of a regenerated humanity (Jer 31:31; Ez 36:27; 37:14; Is 32:15–19; 44:3; Jl 3:1–3; Zec 4:6; 12:10).

From this perspective and in virtue of the parallel passage, Jn 4:10, the "I am thirsty" of Jesus on the cross expresses more of a thirst to give than to receive. As he had offered the Samaritan woman living water, the gift of God which is the Holy Spirit, so now he also offers living water. He thirsts deeply to give the gift of God to all men, delivering to them the Holy Spirit promised in scripture (Ez 36:26ff). This gift is made possible by the fulfillment of his mission and his exaltation on the cross.

"Bowing his head he gave up his spirit" (Jn 19:30)

> After Jesus had taken the vinegar he said, "It is accomplished"; and bowing his head he gave up his spirit. (19:30)

Having said "I am thirsty" and taken the vinegar, Jesus spoke his last word, "It is accomplished." To express this idea precisely, John uses the perfect tense which in Greek indicates the full realization of the work and mission.

The evangelist then solemnly concludes: "And bowing his head he gave up his spirit." Jesus bows his head tranquilly, serenely. He gives his life voluntarily; no one has taken it from him (10:18); and at the same time he gave up his spirit.

Mark and Luke write he "breathed his last" (Mk 15:37; Lk 23:46), and Matthew says he "yielded up his spirit" (Mt 27:50). John, thoughtfully choosing his terms, writes, "he gave up his Spirit."

This expression is deeply significant and has a double value and meaning. The obvious meaning is that Jesus passes away, gives up his soul, dies. In the deeper sense, once his work is finished Jesus gives, hands over, communicates, the Spirit, the gift of his life.

Humanity—in ignorance, but in good faith—offers vinegar to the dying, thirsty Jesus. Jesus accepts it with gratitude, but he, in turn, immediately reciprocates with another gift: He gives the Holy Spirit. Thus the first giving of the Spirit coincides with the majestic moment when Jesus, giving up his life, returns to the Father!

He "pierced his side with a lance; and immediately there came out blood and water" (Jn 19:34).

It was Preparation Day, and to prevent the bodies remaining on the cross during the sabbath—since that sabbath was a day of special solemnity—the Jews asked Pilate to have the legs broken and the bodies taken away. Consequently, the soldiers came and broke the legs of the first man who had been crucified with him and then of the other. When they came to Jesus, they found he was already dead, and so instead of breaking his legs one of the soliders pierced his side with a lance; and immediately there came out blood and water. (19:31–34)

We have here a fact which in the eyes of John is very much a sign. The gesture of the soldier was not necessary, since Jesus was already dead. But the evangelist sees that with the thrust of the lance a word of scripture has been fulfilled: "They will look on the one whom they have pierced" (19:37). Zechariah had written, "But over the House of David and the citizens of Jerusalem I will pour out a spirit of kindness and prayer. They will look on the one whom they have pierced" (Zec 12:10). The literal meaning of that prophetic text is not clear, but the evangelist finds in it a deeper meaning, put there by God: The passage refers to Jesus on the cross, pierced through by a lance. The Book of Revelation alludes to this prophecy in Rv 1:7.

"And immediately there came out blood and water." This phenomenon is explainable medically. One who is crucified stores up blood in the heart. Around the blood accumulates a lymphatic liquid which has the appearance of water. John sees the physical reality but perceives a hidden symbolism in it besides.

The blood. The blood testifies to the reality of the sacrifice of the Lamb which has been offered for the salvation of the world. The blood is also the expression of a debt that has been settled, the price of a ransom, the necessary element for the remission of sin. "The blood of Jesus, his Son, purifies us from all sin" (1 Jn 1:7).

In the Gospel of John the blood of Jesus is also the source of true and eternal life (6:53–54a), eschatological resurrection (6:54b), the true food which gives life (6:55), and the union and mutual permanence of relationship of Jesus and the believer (6:56).

To sum up: In the blood that springs forth from the side of Jesus, the evangelist contemplates the gift which Jesus made of himself on the cross, delivering himself up for love of all men.

In addition, John discreetly alludes to the gift of Jesus' blood which continues to be made in the sacrament of the Eucharist, source of eternal life and mutual union, and pledge of glorious future resurrection.

The water. In the Fourth Gospel, water is a symbol of the Spirit: Jesus is baptized in water, and the Spirit comes to rest upon him (1:32–33). Jesus, filled with the Spirit, has the mission of baptizing in the Holy Spirit (1:33). The new birth is in water which, in baptism, symbolizes the Spirit, operator of that mystery (3:5, 8). The living water promised to the Samaritan woman is the Spirit (4:10, 23). John expressly identifies water with the Spirit (7:37–39).

These things being so, we can see in the water that springs forth from the side of Jesus the symbol of the Spirit who proceeds from the glorified Jesus (19:34). This is a tacit reference to Christian baptism, which is conferred by means of water and the Spirit. "I tell you most solemnly, unless a man is born through water and the Spirit, he cannot enter the kingdom of God" (3:5).

> This is the evidence of one who saw it—trustworthy evidence, and he knows he speaks the truth—and he gives it so that you may believe as well. (19:35)

It is a question, therefore, of solemn testimony. The one who speaks is the mysterious disciple who appears in Jn 19:26–27 as the "disciple he loved." The truth of John's testimony is attested by Jesus himself. And all this has one goal: to invite others to believe in Jesus.

The whole passage harmonizes well with the text of 1 Jn 5:7–8: "There are three witnesses, the Spirit, the water, and the blood, and all three of them agree."

"Receive the Holy Spirit" (Jn 20:21–23)

John had already hinted at the gift of the Spirit at the moment of Jesus' death and at the instant when water flowed forth from his open side (19:28–30, 34). It is not extraordinary, then, that the evangelist would offer us an explicit account of the giving of the Spirit on the Sunday of the Resurrection, once Jesus had been glorified.

The gift of the Spirit was conditional upon the ascension of Jesus to his Father. The evangelist wanted to clearly indicate this ascension by recording the words Jesus speaks to Mary Magdalene: "But go and find the brothers, and tell them: I am ascending to my Father and your Father, to my God and your God" (Jn 20:17b).

When Jesus presents himself to his disciples on Easter afternoon he does so after having been glorified. He then breathes on them, giving them the Holy Spirit.

> He said to them again, "Peace be with you. As the Father sent me, so am I sending you." (Jn 20:21)

Before doing anything else Jesus gives a greeting of peace to the disciples. It is the messianic peace which the prophets announced for future times (Is 9:6; 52:7; Ez 37:26; Zec 9, 10). Jesus the Messiah now gives it to his Apostles.

At once there follows the solemn investiture for the mission. Here Jesus fulfills another of the promises he had made during the Last Supper: "As you sent me into the world, I have sent them into the world" (17:18).

Jesus' words, "As the Father sent me, so am I sending you," are important. By them he creates the apostolic mission of the disciples and of all Christians: to go forth to the spiritual conquest of the world. This mission is supernatural and divine; it proceeds not from human authorities but from Jesus. It is analogous to the mission Jesus received from his Father. The Father is present in all apostolic mission; from his immense love for the world proceeds all of salvation history (see 3:16).

When ecclesiastical authorities act in their official capacities, whether it be to confer baptism, confirmation, sacred orders, or a particular ministry, it is from the Father, Son, and Holy Spirit that these missions to the apostolate proceed.

> After saying this he breathed on them and said: "Receive the Holy Spirit. For those whose sins you forgive, they are forgiven; for those whose sins you retain, they are retained." (20:22–23)

The breath of Jesus is a symbol of a spiritual reality. In the Bible "wind" and "breath" (in Hebrew, *ruah;* and in Greek, *pneuma*) always serve as symbols of the Spirit of God.

The breath of Jesus upon his Apostles signifies that he is giving them the gift of the Holy Spirit as fruit of the saving work the Father entrusted to him (4:34; 6:38–40; 17:4; 19:30). This is the fulfillment of another promise of the master: "It is for your own good that I am going because unless I go, the Advocate will not come to you; but if I do go, I will send him to you" (16:7; see 14:16; 16:13). It is also the fulfillment of the ancient prophecies found in Ez 36:26–27; 37:5–10; Wis 15:11.

With this gift of the Holy Spirit a new creation begins. The breath of Jesus is an echo of the breath of God upon Adam, the man whom he modeled (Gn 2:7).

By virtue of the Spirit which they have received, the Apostles will be able both to pardon and withhold pardon for sins. It is not simply a matter of power to preach the remission of sins; rather, they have received real power to forgive and retain sins. Jesus had already made this known during his life (Mt 18:18). The Council of Trent declared that the Catholic church has always seen in these words the institution of the sacrament of reconciliation (Session XIV, Canon 3).

At first sight the power to forgive sins appears to be a negative action. In actuality, however, the reality hidden in this action is profoundly positive. When the Spirit comes to a person the effect is purification, but at the same time the Spirit infuses in him new, eternal, divine life. This life has its origin in the Father, and it springs forth from Jesus (5:21, 26; 6:54; 10:10).

The Apostles, full of the Holy Spirit, partook of an experience similar to that of Jesus when the Spirit descended to dwell in him in fullness. Because of this transforming anointing they will be able to be like Jesus, the Messiah. Even better, they will be extensions of Jesus, whose mission is summed up in his role as the Lamb of God who takes away the sin of the world and baptizes in the Holy Spirit (see 1:29–34). From this day on, the Apostles will be able to go throughout the world to continue, as servants sent by Jesus, the work that the Father entrusted to his Son, the Anointed of the Spirit.

CHAPTER SIX

"IN THE NAME OF THE FATHER AND OF THE SON AND OF THE HOLY SPIRIT" (MT 28:19)

Meanwhile the eleven disciples set out for Galilee, to the mountain where Jesus had arranged to meet them. When they saw him they fell down before him, though some hesitated. Jesus came up and spoke to them. He said, "All authority in heaven and on earth has been given to me. Go, therefore, make disciples of all the nations; baptize them in the name of the Father and of the Son and of the Holy Spirit, and teach them to observe all the commands I gave you. And know that I am with you always; yes, to the end of time." (28:16–20)

The teaching that Jesus gives to his disciples on the mountain in Galilee consists of four points.
1. Jesus has received all power from the Father, and his sovereignty extends to heaven and earth. He is the Lord of the universe, invested with full, absolute, and universal dominion. Thus we know that his perfect glorification has taken place. He has gone up to heaven and received the kingdom from the hands of God his Father. The gift of the Father is suggested by use of the passive form, "has been given." This is the fulfillment of the enigmatic word Jesus had spoken to the members of the Sanhedrin: "You will see the Son of Man seated at the right hand of the Power..."

(26:64; see also Dn 7:14; Acts 13:33; Rom 1:4; Phil 2:5–11; 1 Tm 3:16).

2. Jesus, the sovereign of the universe, now sends his disciples on a great mission to the whole world. It is this universality, this catholicism which will characterize the church of Christ.

The expression which Matthew uses is particularly eloquent. "Make disciples of all the nations" indicates a move to seriously incorporate the doctrine of the master, Jesus, into the lives of those people the Apostles teach. The Apostles will understand more and more what the universality of the Christian message will mean as they grow in the light of the Spirit.

Jesus limited himself to preaching to the Jews, for this was the order he received from the Father (10:5–6, 23; 15:24). Salvation, however, was destined for all the people of the earth (Is 2:1–5; 42:6; 45:18–20; 49:6). The moment determined by divine providence had arrived in which the new Israel, the authentic remnant, would carry the message of salvation everywhere. Later, all men will be able to be saved by becoming disciples of Jesus.

3. This increase in the number of Jesus' disciples will happen through baptism and teaching. Baptism is the medium through which disciples are added to the number of Jesus' followers. It is an exterior rite, an outward sign by virtue of which a spiritual reality operates in the person who is baptized. Henceforth, the person baptized belongs to God, consecrated to the Father, Son, and Holy Spirit.

In the early years of the church, baptism was received in the name of the Lord Jesus by making an act of surrender to Jesus and believing that from him comes salvation, the forgiveness of sins (Acts 2:38; 4:11; 5:31; 13:23).

The Apostle Paul insists that through baptism the believer is submerged in Christ, who has died and has risen (Rom 6:3ff; Col 2:12). We are sons in the Son (Gal 3:26–27). John refers to baptism by water and the Spirit as a new birth from above (Jn 3:5, 8).

The precision of the baptismal formula found in Matthew, "baptize them in the name of the Father and of the Son and of the Holy Spirit," perhaps reflects the later liturgical use of this phrase in the Christian community. It admirably sets forth an essential aspect of the sacrament: Through baptism a very personal relationship is established between the believer and the Father, Son, and Holy Spirit. He is made able to participate in the love of the Father, the grace of the Lord Jesus, and the communion of the Holy Spirit (2 Cor 13:13).

"Teach them to observe all the commands I gave you." Teaching played a primary role in the ministry of Jesus (see Mt 4:23; 5:2, 19; 7:29; 9:35; 11:1; 13:54). The objective of his teaching was to show how to live ethically and faithfully as sons of God in the kingdom of heaven (5:48).

Matthew devotes numerous pages of his Gospel to recording for Christian posterity the teaching of Jesus and his interpretations of God's law (see 5—7). Similarly, the Gospel of John speaks of the commandments of the Lord (see 13:34; 14:15; 15:10–12).

4. "And know that I am with you always; yes, to the end of time." This promise not only refers to a permanent presence, but to a constant and efficacious help for the messengers of the gospel, especially during persecution. This continuous and working presence is noted in the phrase "I am." The presence of Jesus will remain until the end of time.

With this word, which signals the end of the First Gospel, the risen Jesus fulfills and makes his own the figure and promise of the divine presence constantly presented in the Old Testament: "I will be with you" (see Ex 3:12; Jos 1:5, 9; Jer 1:8; Is 41:10; 43:5). This permanent and efficacious help of Jesus, which transcends time and space, can have no other than a divine origin.

Part II

*The Acts of the Apostles:
The Holy Spirit in the Church*

CHAPTER SEVEN

THE DAWNING OF THE CHURCH

You "Will Be Baptized With the Holy Spirit" (Acts 1:4–8)

In my earlier work, Theophilus, I dealt with everything Jesus had done and taught from the beginning until the day he gave his instructions to the Apostles he had chosen through the Holy Spirit, and was taken up to heaven. He had shown himself alive to them after his Passion by many demonstrations: for forty days he had continued to appear to them and tell them about the kingdom of God. (1:1–3)

After Jesus' resurrection and before his ascension to heaven the Holy Spirit, who had filled Jesus and led him step by step throughout his messianic ministry (Lk 3:22; 4:1, 14, 18; 10:21; 11:20), acts in him to impart to the Apostles his final instructions on the kingdom of God which is at hand (see Lk 21:24b, 31-33; 24:46–49).

Jesus is the one who is fully given over to the Spirit. All that he does is the fruit of the productive action of the Spirit.

When he had been at table with them, he had told them not to leave Jerusalem, but to wait there for what the Father had promised. "It is" he had said "what you have heard me speak about: John baptized with water but you, not many days from now, will be baptized with the Holy Spirit." (1:4–5)

This scene recalls the last meeting of the disciples with Jesus as narrated in the Gospel of Luke.

He then opened their minds to understand the scriptures, and he said to them, "So you see how it is written that the Christ would suffer and on the third day rise from the dead, and that, in his name, repentance for the forgiveness of sins would be preached to all the nations, beginning from Jerusalem. You are witnesses to this. And now I am sending down to you what the Father has promised. Stay in the city then, until you are clothed with the power from on high." (Lk 24:45–49)

Jesus' words to the Apostles in Acts 1:4–5 have three intimately linked parts: "not to leave Jerusalem," "to wait there for what the Father had promised," and to "be baptized with the Holy Spirit."

1. The Apostles ought "not to leave Jerusalem," the holy city, which was chosen by God as the point of departure for the message of salvation (Is 2:1–3; Lk 1:5–25). Jerusalem was chosen as the place where Jesus brought to fulfillment the work the Father had entrusted to him (Lk 9:51), and as the center of radiation of the apostolic mission (Acts 1:8).

2. "To wait there for what the Father had promised." But of what does this promise consist? In Lk 24:49 Jesus said, "And now I am sending down to you what the Father has promised," and in Acts 2:33 Peter clarifies the content of this promise: "Now raised to the heights by God's right hand, he has received from the Father the Holy Spirit, who was promised . . ." The promise of the Father is identified with the Holy Spirit. This allusion to the Holy Spirit as a gift, as one sent from the Father in the name of Jesus, constitutes a point of contact with the theology of John with regard to the Spirit, sent by the Father in response to the supplication of Jesus (Jn 14:16–17, 26; 15:26; 16:7).

3. You "will be baptized with the Holy Spirit." With the coming of the Holy Spirit the mission of Jesus will arrive at its completion.

THE DAWNING OF THE CHURCH

> John the Baptist had said, "I baptize you in water . . . but the one who follows me is more powerful than I am . . . He will baptize you with the Holy Spirit and fire" (Mt 3:11; see Mk 1:8; Lk 3:16; Acts 11:16). And this is the crowning point of Jesus' teaching: The disciples will be baptized with the Holy Spirit. Behind the passive verb is hidden the action of God the Father and his Son the Lord Jesus, who is the one who baptizes with the Holy Spirit (Jn 1:32–33).

Not understanding the meaning of Jesus' words, the disciples are thinking of an imminent restoration of the Davidic monarchy; so those who were gathered there asked him, "Lord, has the time come? Are you going to restore the kingdom to Israel?" (Acts 1:6).

As one can see, the Apostles share the common Jewish hope of national liberation and the restoration of the monarchy. The ideal of the kingdom of God which they have in mind is temporal (see Lk 19:11; Mk 10:37).

> He replied, "It is not for you to know times or dates that the Father has decided by his own authority, but you will receive power when the Holy Spirit comes on you, and then you will be my witnesses not only in Jerusalem but throughout Judaea and Samaria, and indeed to the ends of the earth." (1:6–8)

Jesus does not answer the Apostles' question directly. He leaves the restoration of Israel among the secret purposes of the Father, and in place of that concern he directs the attention of the disciples toward another reality, one which will engage them personally in the immediate future: "You will receive power when the Holy Spirit comes on you . . ."

This is a key statement. It shows the direct effect of the outpouring of the Spirit and, consequently, of the baptism in the Holy Spirit which the Apostles are about to receive. This effect consists of two principal elements.

1. The disciples will be clothed with a power coming from on high (Lk 24:49) or, better said, they will receive the Holy Spirit, who is a divine Power, the Power of God. This will therefore be an investiture of power.

The promise of the Holy Spirit descending upon the Apostles naturally evokes the prophecy in which Isaiah announces that the spirit of Yahweh will rest in all its fullness upon the Davidic Messiah (Is 11:1-2). That same Spirit will now come down upon the messianic preachers. Sent by Jesus, the Messiah, who possesses the Spirit of God in fullness, he will come to them (Acts 2:33). By virtue of that infilling of divine power the disciples will be able to proclaim the good news of the kingdom of God. They will preach as Jesus did: full of the Spirit and in the power of the Spirit (see Lk 4:1, 14, 18, 43; Acts 10:38).

2. This power from on high transforms the missionaries into witnesses of the risen Jesus (Lk 24:48; Acts 1:22; 2:43; 3:15; 4:33; 5:32; 10:39, 41; 13:31). Their field of action will be the entire world. The new movement will go out from Jerusalem the city of salvation; it will pass through Judaea and Samaria, and will launch forth "to the ends of the earth" according to the words of the prophet Isaiah: "I will make you the light of the nations so that my salvation may reach to the ends of the earth" (Is 49:6b; see Mt 28:10; Lk 24: 47-49). Acts 1:8 is a synthesis of the entire book: Everything begins in Jerusalem and will end in Rome, where Paul will preach the kingdom of God and bear witness to the Lord Jesus (28:31).

The disciples obeyed the order they had received, and remained in Jerusalem. Luke takes care to give us the complete list of Apostles and then adds: "All these joined in continuous prayer, together with several women, including Mary the mother of Jesus, and with his brothers" (1:14).

The Charismatic Outpouring of the Spirit on Pentecost (Acts 2:1-13)

Introduction: Feast of Weeks, Feast of Renewal of the Covenant

Our feast of Pentecost coincides with the Jewish feast of Weeks (Ex 34:22; Dt 16:10), also called the feast of Harvest (Ex 23:16) or day of the First Fruits (Nm 28:26). The four traditions of the Pentateuch speak of this solemn feast: Elohistic tradition

(Ex 23:14-17), Yahwistic tradition (Ex 34:18-23), Priestly tradition (Lv 23), and Deuteronomical tradition (Dt 16:1-16).

This agricultural festival is Canaanite in origin, and celebrates the beginning of the wheat harvest. After the conquest of Canaan, Israel incorporated the feast into its liturgical calendar. The feasts of Weeks, Unleavened Bread (Passover), and Tabernacles are the three great pilgrimage festivals of Judaism (Dt 16:16). Of the three, the feast of Weeks is the least important.

To properly celebrate the feast, rest and an atmostphere of joy were necessary. The offerings to be presented at that time are described in Lv 23:17-21; Nm 28:27; Dt 16:10ff; 26:2-11. Dt 16:8-9 indicates how and when the festival should be celebrated:

> For six days you shall eat unleavened bread; on the seventh day there shall be an assembly for Yahweh your God; and you must do no work. You are to count seven weeks, counting these seven weeks from the time you begin to put your sickle into the standing corn.

According to the priestly law (Lv 23:15ff) the feast was to be celebrated for a period of seven weeks or fifty days after the sabbath following Passover. Passover was set for the night of the full moon during the first month of the year.

The Sadducees considered the Passover a sabbath and therefore began to count the seven weeks starting then, thus the feast could fall on any day of the week. For their part, the Pharisees used to count the seven weeks beginning after the sabbath which immediately followed Passover. By this method the feast would always fall on a Sunday. The community at Qumran began to count the seven weeks starting after the first sabbath which followed the Passover octave.

The Book of Ruth, which mentions the barley and wheat harvests, was read publicly during the feast of Weeks (Ru 2:17, 23). With the passage of time, the feast of Pentecost was enriched by the commemoration of the Exodus.

According to Ex 19:1 there were sixty days between the departure of the Chosen People from Egypt and their arrival at Sinai. Because of the rough similarity between the duration of this event and the length of the feast it was not difficult to link the festival with the arrival of the Israelites at the holy mountain. Thus Pentecost became the commemoration of the giving of the Law and of the celebration of the Covenant (2 Chr 15:10–13). Passover and Pentecost acquired a strong liturgical unity: liberation from Egypt and promulgation of the divine law. The writings of Qumran are very clear in this regard. The community there renewed the Covenant at Pentecost, which was also the day when new initiates were admitted. Moreover, Dt 9:10 calls the day of the giving of the Law "the day of the assembly" or, in Greek, "the day of the church."

Other interesting connections that help us better understand our celebration of Pentecost are found in Jewish tradition. Philo interprets the "They saw the voices" of Ex 20:18 by saying that this was possible because the voices had taken on the appearance of flames. Some rabbis even insist that these voices had divided into seventy dialects in order for the seventy peoples of the earth to understand the Law (Gn 10).

Baptism in the Holy Spirit (2:1–4)

When the Pentecost day came round, they had all met in one room. (2:1)

This verse gives us the circumstances of the time and place of the coming of the Holy Spirit in solemn and visible form. It was the day of Pentecost (literally "of the Fifty"), the fiftieth day after Passover. The name of "Pentecost" given to the feast of Weeks we already find in Tb 2:1 and 2 Macc 12:32. As we have said, this feast also commemorated the giving of the Law on Sinai and the celebration of the Covenant, the day of the Assembly (Dt 9:10). This is an important fact in view of the theology of this feast which was to develop.

The group was gathered in one room. This was not the assembly of 120 people described in 1:15, but rather the small nucleus of the Apostles with Mary the mother of Jesus, of which 1:14 speaks. This verse depicts a communal union in concord, friendship, and love, and recalls the assembly mentioned in Ex 19:8 which responded as one to accept the Law given at Sinai.

Suddenly they heard what sounded like a powerful wind from heaven, the noise of which filled the entire house in which they were sitting; and something appeared to them that seemed like tongues of fire; these separated. (2:2–3a)

Suddenly, without anyone foreseeing or suspecting, there came a strong, hurricane-like wind from heaven. Given the context immediately prior to this passage, where it was affirmed that Jesus was going to heaven and would send the Holy Spirit, the Power from on high (Lk 24:49; Acts 1:8–10), "from heaven" indicates that the extraordinary phenomenon described here has a divine origin (see Dt 4:36; Lk 3:22). Jesus has gone up to heaven and from there, from where he is, "from heaven," comes this thunderous hurricane, this impetuous *ruah,* symbol of the divine *ruah,* the Holy Spirit, the Power of God, who had been promised (Lk 24:49), and who now has been sent.

The strong wind "filled the entire house." This expression clearly denotes fullness. In the same way, when the theophany came to Moses "the whole mountain shook violently" (Ex 19: 18). It is worth noting that Luke uses the word *pnoe* to designate the wind, reserving the stronger word *pneuma* for the Holy Spirit.

To the acoustical phenomenon is added a visual one, also of divine origin, as can be gathered from the use of the passive verb (see 1:11; 22:43; 24:34). The phenomenon consisted of the appearance of something "that seemed like tongues of fire," which divided. The qualification "that seemed" is important. A little earlier Luke used a similar expression in speaking of the strong wind (2:2). Throughout his work the author uses such constructions in order to nuance the description and supply a standard for correct interpretation (Lk 3:23; 9:14, 28; 22:41, 44, 59; 23:44; Acts 1:15; 2:41; 6:15). The descriptions given here should not be taken in a strictly literal sense; rather, they serve as images which carry a message linked to the symbolism.

Wind and Fire. In the time of Moses, Sinai was witness to thunderings, lightnings, dense clouds, the powerful sound of trumpets, and smoke like that from an oven, because Yahweh had come down in the form of fire (Ex 19:16–20; 33:18–34:9).

In the time of Elijah, Mount Horeb suffered a hurricane so violent that it cracked the mountains; there was a great earthquake, and there was fire. The scene at Horeb echoed the divine apparition made to Moses at the same place (1 Kgs 19:11–12).

In the great theophany of Jesus' transfiguration were united the cosmic elements of the ancient manifestations, and the two biblical characters favored with them (Lk 9:28–36).

Now, on Pentecost, there is also a theophany, but of a particular kind. Luke knew how to employ vigorous images and expressions to describe the outpouring of the Holy Spirit and to manifest its deep meaning.

The roaring like a strong, impetuous wind coming from above was a symbol of the Spirit whom Jesus was sending from heaven as the Power from on high, according to what he had promised (Lk 24:49).

The tongues of fire also symbolize the divine Spirit, purifier and sanctifier, who would fill each one of the disciples of Jesus, and would enable them to bear witness to Jesus in a testimony "as of fire." In biblical symbolism, fire indicates the presence of God (Ex 19:18; 24:17) and is, moreover, an element of fine and penetrating purification (see Is 1:25; 48:18; Zec 13:9; Mal 3:2–3; Lk 3:16).

> ... and came to rest on the head of each of them. They were all filled with the Holy Spirit, and began to speak foreign languages as the Spirit gave them the gift of speech. (2:3b–4)

As in 1 Kgs 19:11–12 the sacred author says that Yahweh was neither in the hurricane-like wind, nor in the earthquake, nor in the fire. Here, in the context of the giving of the Spirit, the wind and fire are only symbols of the real and personal presence of the Holy Spirit.

When Jesus was baptized, heaven opened and the Spirit descended on him in the form of a dove, symbolizing the beginning of a new creation (see Gn 1:2). Now the Spirit descends upon the small community with the same symbolic elements as the events at Sinai in order to indicate that now is born a new people who will live under the norm of a new Law, the Law of the Spirit. The Holy Spirit takes possession of the disciples of Jesus.

Filled with the Spirit, and by his prompting, the disciples began to speak in other tongues. Their power to express themselves in languages different from their own was a gift of the Spirit which had a very definite purpose: to proclaim the glories of God and bear witness to Jesus (1:8) before the Jewish residents of Jerusalem who had come from all parts of the world. They too were to hear the message of the Spirit, for the good news of Jesus was also for them.

Witnesses of Pentecost (2:5–13)

> Now there were devout men living in Jerusalem from every nation under heaven, and at this sound they all assembled, each one bewildered to hear these men speaking his own language. They were amazed and astonished. "Surely" they said "all these men speaking are Galileans? How does it happen that each of us hears them in his own native language? We hear them preaching in our own language about the marvels of God." Everyone was amazed and unable to explain it; they asked one another what it all meant. Some, however, laughed it off. "They have been drinking too much new wine" they said. (2:6–8; 11b–13)

Jerusalem, a cosmopolitan city since ancient times, gathered to herself Jews born in diverse parts of the world. Our text, although not excluding pilgrims who visited the holy city for the feast of Weeks, appears to refer to Jews who were residents of Jerusalem. Luke makes a special point of mentioning those Jews known for their piety, goodness, and fervor (see also Lk 2:25; Acts 8:2; 22:12). The author, in referring to "every nation under heaven," wants to present Jerusalem as the synthesis and symbol of all humanity.

Upon hearing the roar the people gather. The reason for their amazement is neither the wind nor the noise, which have already passed, but the Apostles who, being all Galileans, are proclaiming the marvels of God in the languages of the listeners. The marvels of God are God's saving interventions in human history. In this case they refer to the saving action of God, who has raised Jesus his Son from the dead, has glorified him, and has given him the fullness of his Spirit. Now Jesus, in turn, pours out that same Spirit upon his disciples.

Filled with the Spirit, the disciples begin to bear witness to Jesus by a testimony of fire in the power of the Spirit. Verses 4, 6, 8, and 11b must be interpreted to mean that the Spirit gave the Apostles the charism of xenoglossia (the ability to speak foreign languages) so that they would ba able to communicate the message to their hearers, many of whom did not speak Aramaic as their native tongue. The Apostles, transformed by the outpouring of the Spirit, began to proclaim the testimony of Jesus with the power and the fire that the Holy Spirit gave them.

There were diverse reactions in the face of such a phenomenon. Some people, amazed but open to the light, "asked one another what it all meant." Others, on the other hand, closed to illumination from above, ridiculed the Apostles, saying, "They have been drinking too much new wine."

The giving of the Spirit was accompanied by two exterior signs, the hurricane-like wind and the tongues of fire. The reception of the Spirit by the disciples was followed by two similarly concrete phenomena: the speaking of foreign languages, and the proclaiming of the marvels of God. This proclamation was carried out with special enthusiasm and ecstatic transports which made some people think the Apostles were drunk.

With this series of wonders, perceptible and experienced, the Apostles entered into the mystery that had been prophesied. Jesus had indeed fulfilled his promise. If John had baptized in water, that is, if he had poured water over the believer as an external sign of interior transformation, now Jesus was baptizing in and with the Holy Spirit. He was pouring the power of the Spirit into the hearts of his disciples, first, to transform them interiorly, and then, make them effective witnesses who would carry his name to the ends of the earth (see Lk 3:16; Acts 1:5; Jn 1:33). They were beginning to understand the significance of the words Jesus had spoken to them: You "will be baptized in the Holy Spirit" (1:5).

Reflections

Literary Type. The literary style used by Luke in Acts 2:1-4 is called haggadic midrash. Haggadic midrash is a narrative based on a historical event that has been interpreted theologically and amplified for the sake of edification. It is a theological, literary genre that makes use of references to scripture to express the doctrinal significance of a transcendent fact, inexplicable in itself by purely human concepts or figures.

Historical Event. The historical event which serves as the basis for the midrash of Acts 2:1-4 must have been a strong, spiritual, communal experience on the feast of Weeks. Luke is underlining the importance of that experience by including images taken from biblical tradition in his description: roaring as of a hurricane wind, tongues of fire, the speaking of foreign languages, and the proclamation of the marvels of God with contagious enthusiasm.

The list of peoples. The catalogue of names presented here qualifies the universality of the expression "Jews from every nation under heaven" (2:5).

> Parthians, Medes and Elamites; people from Mesopotamia, Judaea and Cappadocia, Pontus and Asia, Phrygia and Pamphlyia, Egypt and the parts of Libya round Cyrene; as well as visitors from Rome—Jews and proselytes alike—Cretans and Arabs. (2:9-11a)

The listing is meant to show the universality of the apostolic preaching: The whole world is invited to receive the good news of the gospel, by the power of the Holy Spirit.

This enumeration of the peoples of the Mediterranean world, which, in broad lines, goes from east to west and from north to south, was no doubt inspired by an ancient astrological calendar, known because the peoples placed themselves in connection with the signs of the Zodiac and were listed according to its order. Luke adopted this manner of enumeration as an easy description of the "universe" of his time.*

---

*La Biblia de Jerusalén (Bilbao: Desclée de Brouwer, 1975), p. 1551.

The phenomenon of xenoglossia, a charism of the Holy Spirit, invites one to consider how the unity of humanity, broken long ago at the tower of Babel (Gn 11:1-9), may now be recovered by means of the preaching of the gospel, carried to the ends of the earth thanks to the influence of the Holy Spirit (Acts 1:1; Mt 28:29).

Testimony of Peter with the Eleven (Acts 2:14-36)

Ordinarily the first discourse of Peter is spoken about without much attention being given Luke's reference to the eleven other Apostles. Nevertheless, this reference is important: When Peter speaks he is not portrayed as being alone, but with the Eleven. If the Eleven speak, it is Peter who is presented as chief and head of the apostolic body. The testimony of Peter is that of all his brothers and is the first apostolic testimony about Jesus in the power and fire of the Spirit.

The testimony consists of two parts. In the first, begun by the address "Men of Judaea," Peter gives the true interpretation of what happened on that Pentecost morning: It was the fulfillment of the prophecy of Joel concerning the outpouring of the Holy Spirit (Acts 2:14-23). In the second part, divided into two sections by the words "Men of Israel" and "Brothers," Peter bears witness to Jesus for the first time (2:22-35). The testimony ends with a solemn declaration of faith (2:36).

The Outpouring of the Spirit (2:14-21)

Through the mouth of Peter, the Holy Spirit bears witness to his own work. Peter's words explain what is happening. God is beginning to fulfill that which he himself had announced through his prophet Joel. He has now poured out his Spirit upon the Apostles and will continue to pour it out in profusion, not only upon them but upon all mankind: men and women, young and old, slave and free. This presence of the Spirit will be manifested by various charismatic gifts: prophecies, visions, dreams, miracles, and signs (Jl 3:1-5).

"All who call on the name of the Lord will be saved" (2:21). Peter now applies this promise to Jesus. He who calls upon the name of the Lord Jesus will attain salvation. This reference allows Peter to shift to giving testimony explicitly about Jesus.

Testimony about Jesus (2:22–35)

The testimony that Peter and the Eleven give of Jesus, in the power and fire of the Holy Spirit, is of the greatest importance: It contains the basic elements of the good news. This testimony is not a discourse, but a proclamation, that is, a *kerygma,* a gospel, a happy announcement. Four fundamental points make up this gospel *kerygma:*

Jesus, prophet (2:22). Peter's testimony begins by giving Jesus the title "Jesus of Nazareth," underlining his condition as man, showing him to be our brother who lived among us, like us, with all our limitations except sin (Jn 8:46; Heb 4:15).

This Jesus of Nazareth was a man accredited by God through miracles, signs, and wonders. It was God who worked these marvels through him for the benefit of man. Jesus was one sent by God, a charismatic prophet. God the Father anointed him with the Holy Spirit and with power in order to bring the kingdom of heaven (see Lk 3:22; 4:1, 14, 18–21; Acts 10:38).

Dead on the cross (2:23). Jesus was delivered up to death on a cross. The Jews were the ones responsible for his death, although the actual crucifixion was carried out at the hands of pagans. Given that the people listening to Peter were not the ones directly responsible for Jesus' death, we can see in Peter's "you killed him" the men of all times. We ourselves are among them. In the final analysis, however, Jesus died on the cross by the "deliberate intention and foreknowledge of God," who desired that his Son should die in order to bring Israel to repentance and the forgiveness of sins (see Jn 3:16; Acts 5:31).

Raised up by God (2:24–32). God resurrected this Jesus, descendant of David, freeing him from death. The mystery of the resurrection was foretold by the prophet-king David when he wrote of the future Anointed: You will not "allow your holy one to experience corruption" (Acts 2:27b). And Peter adds, "All of us are witnesses to that" (2:32b). The disciples of Jesus had, in fact, experienced their risen master. For forty days he had appeared to them and spoken of the kingdom of God (see 1:3). The Apostles are qualified witnesses of the risen Jesus; they tell what they saw and heard.

Glorified, filled with the Spirit (2:33–35). Once resurrected, Jesus was exalted by the sovereign power of God. Peter emphasizes this:

> Now raised to the heights by God's right hand, he has received from the Father the Holy Spirit, who was promised, and what you see and hear is the outpouring of that Spirit. (2:33)

This is the crowning point of the message, the substance of the mystery of Pentecost. As the supreme gift of his glorification Jesus received from the Father—according to his promise—the gift of the Holy Spirit. Jesus, in turn, poured it out upon his disciples so that the church might open itself to life, the new People of God be born, and the ancient prophecies be fulfilled. He did this so that the New Covenant could be written upon their hearts, remaining sealed forever in all its fullness (see Jer 31:31–33; Ez 36:27; Is 59:21).

Peter cites a prophecy of David in which Jesus' exaltation is foretold: "The Lord said to my Lord: Sit at my right hand until I make your enemies a footstool for you" (Acts 2:34b–35).

Solemn Declaration of Faith (2:36)

With this verse we see how Jesus reached the culmination of his messianic mission and fulfilled in himself, in all completeness, the plan which the Father had conceived from all eternity: to send his Son to earth. Peter ended his testimony with this solemn declaration of faith:

> For this reason the whole house of Israel can be certain that God has made this Jesus whom you crucified both Lord and Christ. (2:36)

The mystery of Jesus is summed up in three words which will be the object of faith for all believers. The risen and glorified Jesus is Savior, Messiah, and Lord.

Savior. "Jesus" (in Hebrew, Yeshua or Joshua) means "Yahweh saves." Jesus is the salvation of God foretold by the prophets (Is 45:8; 51:5; 56:1). Jesus is *the* savior: He is the savior of the world who comes to free the world from sin (Mt 1:21; Lk 2:11; Jn 4:42).

Messiah. Jesus is the Messiah, the Christ, the Anointed of the Spirit (Is 11:1; 42:1; 61:1). From the moment of his virginal conception, Jesus was the Messiah, full of the Spirit (Lk 1:35). With this gift of the Holy Spirit to his Son's glorified human nature, the Father establishes Jesus as "Messiah-Christ" in all his fullness. Overflowing with the Spirit, Jesus can and wishes to give, pour out, and baptize in the Holy Spirit (Jn 1:33; 7:39; 16:7).

Lord. God has made Jesus "Lord"; he has made him his royal heir and has given him "all authority in heaven and on earth" (Mt 28:18). Jesus is the Lord of all humanity and of the entire universe, since everything belongs to God.

In the Old Testament the title of "Lord" is given only to God (Is 45:23). On now being applied to Jesus, this title affirms that Jesus is above all created beings, and is divine. Jesus is the Son of God; he is God himself (see 1 Cor 12:3; 2 Cor 4:5; Phil 2:11; Rom 9:5; 10:9; Col 2:6; Jn 20:28).

The confession of Jesus as Savior, Messiah, and Lord is an essential tenet of the Christian faith. Providentially, it has remained wedged in the solemn formula with which liturgical prayers are ordinarily concluded: "We ask it through Jesus Christ, your Son, our Lord...."

The Book of Acts presents many other discourses by important figures of the early church: Peter, Stephen, Paul (3:12–26; 4:8–12, 19–22; 5:29–32; 7:1–53; 10:34–43; 13:16–41; 4:14–18; 15:7–11, 13–21; etc.). All these discussions fall more or less into the category of testimonies to Jesus inspired by the Holy Spirit. These testimonies will not be the direct object of our study; we will only refer to portions of them where mention of the Holy Spirit explicitly appears.

The Birth of the Church, Creation of the Spirit
(Acts 2:37–41)

When Peter, with the force and fire of the Spirit, had given the interpretation of the events of that Pentecost and had borne witness to Jesus, the sharers were touched to the heart. Opening up to grace, they responded to the intimate action of God. They said to Peter and the other Apostles:

> "What must we do, brothers?" "You must repent," Peter answered "and every one of you must be baptized in the name of Jesus Christ for the forgiveness of your sins, and you will receive the gift of the Holy Spirit. The promise that was made is for you and your children, and for all those who are far away, for all those whom the Lord our God will call to himself." (2:37–39)

Peter's words contain the elements of Christian initiation: conversion, baptism in the name of Jesus, the gift of the Holy Spirit.

Conversion. The first thing that must be done is turn to God through a profound interior conversion, abandoning sin and all that is connected with it. With this invitation Peter follows the example of Jesus, who began his messianic career with that inaugural cry: "The time has come . . . and the kingdom of God is close at hand. Repent, and believe the Good News" (Mk 1:15).

Baptism in the name of Jesus. This baptism is ordained for the forgiveness of sins. It is a rite of purification which is given in the name of Jesus the Messiah or received while invoking his name. This baptism is both an act of consecration and an act of incorporation through faith into Jesus, who has died, risen from the dead, and is now glorified (Acts 5:31; 8:16; 10:48; 19:5; 22:16; Rom 4:25; 6:3–4; Col 2:12–13; Eph 2:4–7).

The gift of the Holy Spirit. Once converted and baptized in the name of Jesus, the new believers receive the gift of the Holy Spirit, the gift God himself has promised. The Holy Spirit, emphasizes Peter, is not solely for the Apostles, but for all those who accept the Apostles' testimony. Furthermore, this gift is extended to their children and to all those whom the Lord calls. The promise of the

Holy Spirit is offered, then, to the Jews and Gentiles of all places and times. Only in this way can the good news be carried from Jerusalem to the ends of the earth. And this can take place only under the powerful action of the Holy Spirit.

Luke comments:

> He spoke to them for a long time using many arguments, and he urged them, "Save yourselves from this perverse generation." They were convinced by his arguments, and they accepted what he said and were baptized. That very day about three thousand were added to their number. (2:40–41)

The number "three thousand" shows the wonderful fruit of the outpouring of the Holy Spirit. Magnificent harvest of the Spirit! In a moment the Holy Spirit has transformed the hearts of that multitude and brought to birth in them faith in Jesus, Lord and Messiah. They decided to change their lives, renounce sin, turn to the Lord, and be consecrated and incorporated into Jesus through baptism. The Holy Spirit, gift and promise of the Father, descended upon them all. And Jesus continued the work he had just begun; he continued baptizing in the Holy Spirit.

"Peter, filled with the Holy Spirit" (Acts 4:8)

The Holy Spirit was sent by Jesus to transform the disciples into effective witnesses for him (1:8; Jn 15:26–27; 16:7–11).

After Peter and John had, in the name of Jesus, worked the healing of a man crippled from birth (3:1–10) and proclaimed before the people of Israel their faith in Jesus—the holy one, the righteous one, and prince who leads to life, the servant of God who died on the cross and rose again (3:11–25)—the Temple guards laid hands on the Apostles and threw them into prison. The following day they were brought before the Sanhedrin. Placed in their midst, the Apostles were asked, "By what power, and by whose name have you men done this?"

> Then Peter, filled with the Holy Spirit, addressed them, "Rulers of the people, and elders! If you are questioning us today about

an act of kindness to a cripple, and asking us how he was healed, then I am glad to tell you all, and would indeed be glad to tell the whole people of Israel, that it was by the name of Jesus Christ the Nazarene, the one you crucified, whom God raised from the dead, by this name and by no other that this man is able to stand up perfectly healthy, here in your presence, today. This is the stone rejected by you the builders, but which has proved to be the keystone. For of all the names in the world given to men, this is the only one by which we can be saved." (4:8–12)

It is interesting to note that in the original Greek, Luke uses not simply the word "filled," but the passive construction "having been filled" to describe Peter. This form puts into relief the action of the Holy Spirit upon the Apostles at the very moment when such action was required. Peter experiences a release of the Holy Spirit in order to proclaim the testimony of Jesus with *parresia,* that is, with courage, audacity, frankness, and ease of speech before people of higher rank.

Peter's brief testimony before the leaders of the people and the elders touches these points: 1) The Jews crucified the Messiah, Jesus of Nazareth; 2) God raised him from the dead; 3) he is "the stone rejected by the builders that proved to be the keystone" (Ps 118:22); 4) "Of all the names in the world given to men, this is the only one by which we can be saved" (4:12).

Jesus alone is the savior (5:31; 13:23). Salvation, foretold and prefigured in the Old Testament (2:21; 7:25; 13:47), will be the central question in the crisis narrated in Acts 15. That salvation was proclaimed by the apostolic preaching (11:14; 13:26) for all men (13:47) through faith (16:30ff).

New Outpouring of the Spirit (Acts 4:23–31)

As soon as Peter and John were set free they went to their brothers and sisters and told them all that had been said to them by the high priests and elders (4:23). Luke uses this occasion to offer us a beautiful example of the early Christian community gathered in prayer.

The passage presents two pictures: the assembly directing a prayer to God (4:24b–30), and the Holy Spirit filling all those who are present (4:31).

Prayer of the Community (4:24–30)

The first part of the prayer is an appeal to God, creator of heaven and earth and proclaimer of the messianic future:

> "Master," they prayed "it is you who made heaven and earth and sea, and everything in them; you it is who said through the Holy Spirit and speaking through our ancestor David, your servant: Why this arrogance among the nations, these futile plots among the peoples? Kings on earth setting out to war, princes making an alliance, against the Lord and against his Anointed." (4:24b–26)

It is from God that revelation comes. The Holy Spirit uses human instruments, in this case David, to communicate the message. Luke had already referred to the Holy Spirit as the source of prophecy in 1:16, when speaking of the treachery of Judas.

In a literal sense, the author of the psalm speaks of a coalition of pagan kings against Yahweh and the king of Israel, the Anointed of God. The author of Acts finds in this passage a deeper meaning and freely interprets it in relation to Jesus.

The Anointed is now "your holy servant Jesus" (4:30), the Anointed of the Spirit. The kings and rulers who have allied themselves against Jesus are Herod and Pontius Pilate. The nations are the pagans; the peoples are the Jews. In coming together against Jesus these enemies are merely instruments, so that what God had already predetermined in his power and wisdom would be fully realized (see 2:23).

Only the Holy Spirit, the one who had inspired the psalm, could reveal the second, deeper meaning which he had put there.

The second part of the prayer is a supplication, a fervent plea with a view to the proclamation of the word:

**La traduction oecuménique de la Bible* (Paris: Les Editions du Cerf—Les Bergers et les Mages, 1972), p. 372.

> And now, Lord, take note of their threats and help your servants to proclaim your message with all boldness, by stretching out your hand to heal and to work miracles and marvels through the name of your holy servant Jesus. (4:29–30)

The community implores God on behalf of the Apostles, the servants of God, for the power to proclaim the word with all boldness and freedom, and the power to work healings, signs, and wonders in the name of Jesus. Having done this, the believers ask God to confirm the apostolic preaching with the same signs that had accompanied the preaching of Jesus himself (see 2:22; Mk 1:34; 6:7–13; 16:17–18).

Outpouring of the Spirit (4:31)

> As they prayed, the house where they were assembled rocked; they were all filled with the Holy Spirit and began to proclaim the word of God boldly. (4:31)

This gift of the Spirit recalls the wonder of Pentecost (2:1–4). Here, the shaking of the place where they were meeting replaces the hurricane-like wind. The Holy Spirit is always present in the Christian community, communicating his force and his power in order to continue the mission of bearing witness to Jesus. Thus the author comments that they "began to proclaim the word of God boldly."

To "lie to the Holy Spirit" (Acts 5:3)

This story describes the attempt of Ananias and Sapphira to deceive the Apostles. The two of them wanted to create the impression among the brethren that they were divesting themselves of the entire sum of money they had received in the sale of their property. In reality, however, they had kept back a part. Through direct revelation Peter discovers the lie and says to Ananias, "How can Satan have so possessed you that you should lie to the Holy Spirit and keep back part of the money from the land?" (5:3). And he adds, "It is not to man that you have lied, but to God" (5:4c).

A bit later he says to Sapphira, "So you and your husband have agreed to put the Spirit of the Lord to the test!" (5:9a). As punishment, the two of them fell dead, one after the other (5:5a, 10a).

The sin of Ananias and Sapphira consisted of having wished, for love of money, to deceive the Apostles, and through them the Holy Spirit present in their brothers and sisters. The Spirit immediately entered into action with the rigor of a power sovereignly present in the midst of the community.

The punishment filled all who heard of it with fear; it was now clear that no one could deceive God or those God establishes as leaders of the Christian community with impunity.*

The authentic sharing of goods among the brethren did not spring from a simple decision of the will, but from a supernatural inspiration of the Spirit. To want to trick the Apostles through the exercise of false charismatic gifts is equivalent to wanting to deceive the Holy Spirit. It was Satan, the tempter, the father of lies, who intervened with his nefarious influence (see Lk 22:3; Jn 13:2, 27).

The Testimony of the Apostles and the Spirit (Acts 5:32)

> In reply Peter and the Apostles said, "Obedience to God comes before obedience to men; it was the God of our ancestors who raised up Jesus, but it was you who had him executed by hanging him on a tree. By his own right hand God has now raised him up to be leader and savior, to give repentance and forgiveness of sins through him to Israel. We are witnesses to all this, we and the Holy Spirit whom God has given to those who obey him." (5:29–32)

The Apostles are conscious of the fulfillment of Jesus' promise. He had promised to send them the Spirit in order to empower them to be his witnesses. The testimony of the Apostles and the Spirit is one and one alone (see Mt 10:20; Lk 12:12; Jn 7:39; 14:26; 15:26–27; Acts 1:8; 4:32).

---

*La Biblia de Jerusalén, p. 1556.

CHAPTER EIGHT

THE FIRST COMMUNITIES

Men "filled with the Spirit and with wisdom"
(Acts 6:3,5)

As the number of disciples grew, the Apostles soon saw themselves overextended in their pastoral work, both in spiritual and material duties.

At one point the Jewish Christians who lived in Jerusalem, but whose mother tongue was Greek and who were originally of the Diaspora, felt that their needy widows were not being sufficiently attended to in the daily distribution of food. This material service must have been carried out first by the Apostles, and then by the presbyters of Jerusalem. In the face of complaints by these Hellenist–Jewish Christians the Apostles made this decision:

> "You, brothers, must select from among yourselves seven men of good reputation, filled with the Spirit and with wisdom; we will hand over this duty to them, and continue to devote ourselves to prayer and to the service of the word." The whole assembly approved of this proposal and elected Stephen, a man full of faith and of the Holy Spirit, together with Philip, Prochorus, Nicanor, Timon, Parmenas, and Nicolaus of Antioch, a

convert to Judaism. They presented these to the Apostles who prayed and laid their hands on them. (6:3–6)

This group consisted of seven men. The number "seven," besides being the symbol of perfection and fullness, recalls the council of government and administration of each city. According to Josephus Flavius these councils were made up of seven judges.

The team was probably formed of Christians chosen from among the Hellenist Jews. They were required to be "of good reputation, filled with the Spirit and with wisdom." These qualities were already considered essential for leaders under the Mosaic Law (Ex 18:21; Nm 27:18; Dt 1:13). The term "Spirit" does not necessarily designate the Holy Spirit, but in view of the general context of the book and the explicit mention of the Holy Spirit in Acts 6:5; 7:51, 55, it probably does.

The people were directed to choose this group of seven men. Nevertheless, it was up to the Apostles to establish them in their new ministry by means of prayer and the laying on of hands. "This gesture was a traditional one in Judaism for expressing installation, with transmission of the Spirit, in a position over the community. The Twelve could also find support for this practice in the Pentateuch (Nm 27:18; Dt 34:9)"*

Thus the Apostles, freed of these material concerns, would be able to devote themselves "to prayer and to the service of the word." This would seem to indicate that the ministry of the Seven was viewed as a material service. But by what we shall see in regard to Stephen and Philip (Acts 6:8–7:60; 8:4–40; 21:8) the service of this group was not limited only to concerns of a practical nature. The work of the Seven was a genuine participation in the apostolic charism, which placed primary importance upon preaching of the word.

The Seven constituted a Judeo-Hellenist organization parallel to that of the Judeo-Hebrews; they took material and spiritual responsibility for the Christian community of the Hellenists.

---

*André Lemaire, *Les ministères aux origines de l'Eglise*, in *Lectio Divina* 68 (Paris: Les Editions du Cerf, 1971), p. 57.

"This moment was important in the development of the church: Part of the Christian community in Jerusalem ceases to be under the direct government of the Hebrews; the Hellenist community becomes autonomous."*

Stephen, a Man Full of Faith and the Holy Spirit
(Acts 6:5,8,10; 7:55)

The author of Acts gives an important place in his work to Stephen (6:1–8:2). At various times he refers to the Holy Spirit, who filled Stephen and inspired him to speak. Stephen is a witness to Jesus the Messiah, anointed by the power and fire of the Spirit.

The assembly chooses Stephen for ministry among the Hellenist Christians because he was "man full of faith and of the Holy Spirit" (6:5). Moreover, he was "filled with grace and power and began to work miracles and great signs among the people" (6:8). Stephen is therefore described as a man full of charismatic gifts, manifestations of the Spirit.

The Hellenists of the Synagogue of Freedmen began to dispute with Stephen, but "they found they could not get the better of him because of his wisdom, and because it was the Spirit that prompted what he said" (6:10). This was nothing but the fulfillment of one of Jesus' promises (Lk 21:15; Acts 1:8).

Acts offers us one of Stephen's discourses (7:2–53), which is the longest discourse in the entire book. It is a testimony, filled with the power and wisdom of the Spirit. It presents the history of Israel from Abraham to Solomon and the construction of the Temple. It lingers especially on Moses, who is viewed as a type of Jesus (7:17–43), and then passes rapidly to a denunciation of Israel: "You stubborn people, with your pagan hearts and pagan ears. You are always resisting the Holy Spirit, just as your ancestors used to do" (7:51). The resistance of the Israelites to the Holy Spirit was manifested in their opposition to Moses (Nm 27:14; Is 63:10) and, in general, to the prophets through whom the Holy Spirit spoke. Now their resistance to the Spirit is manifested in their rejection of the heralds of the gospel.

―――――――
Ibid.

Led before the Sanhedrin and accused by false witnesses, Stephen is suddenly transfigured. "The members of the Sanhedrin all looked intently at Stephen, and his face appeared to them like the face of an angel"(6:15). This was because Stephen,

> filled with the Holy Spirit, gazed into heaven and saw the glory of God, and Jesus standing at God's right hand. "I can see heaven thrown open" he said "and the Son of Man standing at the right hand of God." (7:55–56)

The Holy Spirit who had given Stephen faith, grace, power, and wisdom now enabled him to contemplate, in an ecstatic vision, Jesus, the Son of Man, in the glory of God. His transfiguration was the effect and reflection of his vision.

The Gift of the Spirit in Samaria (Acts 8:14–18)

In order to understand more exactly the passage on Philip, the evangelist of Samaria (8:5–13), it is helpful to be acquainted with the historical position of the church at this time.

> That day a bitter persecution started against the church in Jerusalem, and everyone except the Apostles fled to the country districts of Judaea and Samaria. Those who had escaped went from place to place preaching the Good News. (8:1,4)

In the course of the Acts of the Apostles the gospel is going to cross the frontiers of Jerusalem and go out to the entire world. Luke tells us in brief that the towns of Judaea and Samaria received the gospel message, and then fixes his attention on the evangelization of a town in Samaria by Philip, one of the seven Hellenist deacons. This city could be Sychar or another such village (Jn 4:5). Some manuscripts read, "the city of Samaria." If this rendering were the original one, Luke would be thinking of Sebaste, the new Hellenist Samaria built by Herod the Great. This would highlight Luke's insight that Samaria is like another Jerusalem, on the verge of receiving the gift of the Spirit (2:37–39).

Philip preaches Jesus the Messiah:

The people united in welcoming the message Philip preached, either because they had heard of the miracles he worked or because they saw them for themselves. There were, for example, unclean spirits that came shrieking out of many who were possessed, and several paralytics and cripples were cured. As a result there was great rejoicing in that town. When they believed Philip's preaching of the Good News about the Kingdom of God and the name of Jesus Christ, they were baptized, both men and women. (8:6–8, 12)

Like Stephen, Philip was a "man full of faith and of the Holy Spirit" (6:5). He was charismatic. The wonders he performed were works of power, perceptible signs of the power of the Spirit, who was present to confirm the testimony of the evangelist. Even a magician named Simon, who for a long time had amazed the inhabitants of the region with his magical arts, embraced the faith and was baptized. He stayed with Philip and was amazed upon seeing the signs and great miracles which he performed.

When the Apostles in Jerusalem heard that Samaria had accepted the word of God, they sent Peter and John to them, and they went down there, and prayed for the Samaritans to receive the Holy Spirit, for as yet he had not come down on any of them: they had only been baptized in the name of the Lord Jesus. Then they laid hands on them, and they received the Holy Spirit. (8:14–17)

As we have said, for the author of Acts (the city of) Samaria was like a second Jerusalem which, upon accepting the preaching of the kingdom of God and believing in the name of Jesus the Messiah, would also receive the gift of the Spirit. What happened in Jerusalem should happen wherever the gospel is preached and accepted.
But an important detail: If the proclamation of the gospel was to go out from Jerusalem (Lk 24:47–48; Acts 1:8), the Apostles, who were personal witnesses of the death and resurrection of Jesus and first beneficiaries of the Spirit (1:5; 2:14), would have to be vigilant that the gospel preserve its purity and authenticity. Therefore, on finding out that Samaria had accepted the word of God,

the Apostles at Jerusalem sent representatives of the apostolic college to visit this newly born community in order to verify the quality of its faith (9:32). Peter and John, who appear together in the first days after Pentecost (3:1, 11; 4:13), are also found here, in the first instance of evangelistic expansion. The apostolic college appears to have been responsible for evangelization as a whole.

Upon arriving in Samaria, Peter and John found that the Holy Spirit "had not come down on any of them: they had only been baptized in the name of the Lord Jesus" (8:16). The Apostles prayed for them, laid hands on them, and the Samaritans received the Holy Spirit. But how is it possible that the Samaritans had not received the gift of the Holy Spirit, as Luke affirms in 2:37–39, if they had been baptized in the name of Jesus the Messiah?

The answers that have been given to solve this problem are not wholly satisfactory. Some mystery will always remain. It is thought that the Samaritans, on being baptized, did in fact receive the internal gift of the Spirit, but not the charismatic manifestations of his presence. Upon their arrival Peter and John became aware of this want, and prayed for them at once with the laying on of hands. The Holy Spirit then fell upon the Samaritans. The reaction of Simon the magician would seem to indicate that perceptible manifestations of the Spirit immediately followed (8:18–19).

I believe that Luke has certain goals in mind in offering this passage. The description of the evangelization of Samaria does not appear to be principally oriented toward teaching who are the authorized ministers of the gift of the Spirit. The doctrinal purpose seems different. The passage stresses instead that the apostolic college, and especially Peter, has the duty of overseeing the authenticity and unity of the faith. The Apostles were qualified witnesses of the life, death, and resurrection of Jesus (1:21–22) and were established by him as the twelve princes of the new Israel (Lk 6:12–15; 22:28–30; Acts 1:13–16). Therefore, they are the ones clearly responsible for the evangelistic mission (see 9:32; 10:12; 15:7–12).

The account of the evangelization of Samaria is also intended to stress that, besides baptism in the name of Jesus the Messiah, the outpouring of the Spirit is an indispensible element for being a full disciple of Christ. The active presence of the Spirit should be manifested exteriorly, through his gifts and charisms. This passage is a diptych built on the fundamental theme of the baptism and gift of the Holy Spirit.

Baptism in the name of Jesus the Messiah (2:38a). Philip preaches Christ and announces the kingdom of God. He does signs, casts out unclean spirits, and works healings. Many men and women, including a magician, are baptized.

Charismatic outpouring of the Holy Spirit (2:38b). Peter and John come, pray over the baptized, lay hands on them, and the Holy Spirit falls upon them. The work of Christianization is complete. They have been made full disciples of Christ. Throughout the Book of Acts, Luke emphasizes the charismatic gifts of the Holy Spirit. (see 2:1–4; 8:14–24; 10:44–48; 11:15–17; 19:1–7).

The episode of Simon the Magician also has certain purpose.

> When Simon saw that the Spirit was given through the imposition of hands by the Apostles, he offered them some money. "Give me the same power" he said "so that anyone I lay my hands on will receive the Holy Spirit." Peter answered, "May your silver be lost forever, and you with it, for thinking that money could buy what God has given for nothing!" (8:18–20)

A likely purpose for recording this interchange is to combat, right from the beginning, some possible abuses of the charismatic gifts. The charisms, manifestations of the Spirit for the good and edification of the community, are free gifts that come from the Spirit—who is himself the Gift of God—and cannot be bought or bartered for.

Philip, at the Disposal of the Holy Spirit
(Acts 8:26,29,39).

Luke offers us another story about Philip the evangelist (8:26–40). Philip, a man full of the Spirit and wisdom, is a willing instrument of the Spirit.

Philip appeared to be in Jerusalem when the angel of the Lord came to him. The angel ordered him to take the road to Gaza. Philip did so and saw an Ethiopian eunuch seated in his carriage and reading one of the Servant Songs of the prophet Isaiah:

Like a sheep that is led to the slaughter-house, like a lamb that is dumb in front of its shearers, like these he never opens his mouth. He has been humiliated and has no one to defend him. Who will ever talk about his descendants, since his life on earth has been cut short! (8:32–33)

The Spirit said to Philip, "Go up and meet that chariot" (8:29). Philip ran and asked the Ethiopian, "Do you understand what you are reading?" He answered, "How can I . . . unless I have someone to guide me?" So he invited Philip to get in and sit by his side (8:30–31).

Philip then told him the good news of Jesus, starting with the text in Isaiah. The Ethiopian official accepted the message and believed in Jesus. When they arrived at a place where there was water the Ethiopian said, "Look, there is some water here; is there anything to stop me from being baptized?" Inserted in the Western Text of the passage at this point is a very ancient liturgical gloss: "And Philip said, 'If you believe with all your heart, you may.' And he replied, 'I believe that Jesus Christ is the Son of God'" (8:37). And Philip baptized him.

The Alexandrian Codex and some of the Fathers present an interesting variation here. They write, "The Holy Spirit fell on the eunuch . . ." The gift of the Spirit follows on faith and baptism in the name of Jesus the Messiah for the forgiveness of sins. At that moment the Ethiopian had been baptized in the Spirit, had received the messianic baptism, and had been incorporated into Christian community. "After they had come up out of the water again, Philip was taken away by the Spirit of the Lord and the eunuch never saw him again but went on his way rejoicing" (8:39). This kind of "abduction" was frequent in the lives of the ancient prophets (see 1 Kgs 18:12; 2 Kgs 2:9–12:6; Ez 3:14; 8:3; 11:24; 43:5; Dn 14:36).

The story ends by saying, "Philip found that he had reached Azotus and continued his journey proclaiming the good news in every town as far as Caesarea" (8:40). Years later, when Paul and Luke pass through Caesarea they will find this evangelist still there (21:8).

The story of Philip and the Ethiopian shows that the Holy Spirit is the soul and principal mover of evangelization. The Holy Spirit is the one who calls to faith. Philip is his obedient instrument and, moved by his power, he goes wherever the Spirit takes him. Philip is a tireless proclaimer of the gospel.

Ananias, Instrument of the Spirit for Paul (Acts 9:17)

Luke mentions the Holy Spirit in recounting the calling of Paul. When Ananias, obeying the order of Jesus, had entered the house where Saul was he laid hands on him and said:

> Brother Saul, I have been sent by the Lord Jesus who appeared to you on your way here so that you may recover your sight and be filled with the Holy Spirit. (9:17)

The imposition of hands is a gesture used in praying for healing of Saul's sight (see Lk 4:40; 13:13; Acts 9:12; 28:8) and for the outpouring of the Spirit upon him (6:6; 8:17–18; 13:3; 19:6).

The expression "be filled with the Holy Spirit," a passive form, is characteristic of Luke. It designates an outpouring of the prophetic Spirit, the Spirit who gives the impulse to speak words under divine inspiration (Lk 1:15, 41, 67; Acts 2:4; 4:8, 31; 13:9; see Lk 4:1; Acts 6:3, 5; 7:55; 11:22).

As Saul had been chosen by the Lord as an instrument for bringing the good news to both the Gentiles and the kings and sons of Israel (9:15), he also must receive the outpouring of the Spirit. Jesus promised this Spirit to the Twelve to enable them to be his witnesses to the ends of the earth (1:8).

The author of Acts comments, "Immediately it was as though scales fell from Saul's eyes and he could see again. So he was baptized there and then" (9:18). Once again Luke, without insisting on a logical order in the elements, emphasizes that baptism and the gift of the Spirit are realities which go together to make up a Christian. Where there is baptism in the name of Jesus, there should also be an outpouring of the Spirit (2:38; 8:14–17; 19:7). The converse is also true: Where the Spirit reveals his active presence through charismatic manifestations, it is necessary to administer baptism in the name of Jesus (9:18; 10:44–48; 11:15–18).

The Church Increases with the Help of the Spirit (Acts 9:31)

In a descriptive summary rich in content Luke describes the church or churches of Palestine enjoying peace and growing under the inspiration of the Spirit:

> The churches throughout Judaea, Galilee and Samaria were now left in peace, building themselves up, living in the fear of the Lord, and filled with the consolation of the Holy Spirit. (9:31)

"Churches" here means the sum total of the Christian communities in that area (20:28). In the Old Testament the Greek term *ecclesia* referred to the assembly of the chosen people, especially in the desert (Ex 19:7–15; Dt 9:10; 10:4). The author of the Book of Acts uses the word "church" to designate the group of first believers in Jerusalem, gathered in "one communion, born of the apostolic witness, centered in faith in the risen Jesus, and animated by the Holy Spirit."*

The churches "were building themselves up." This expression is a metaphor, Pauline style, which serves to express growth in the Christian life. The church was building itself up, or raising itself as a building goes up, aspiring to reach total perfection (1 Thes 5:11; 1 Cor 8:1; 10:23; 14:3–5, 12, 17, 26).

The churches were "living in the fear of the Lord." They were living in accord with what pleased God, fulfilling his will and

---

*La traduction oecuménique de la Bible, p. 374.

observing his commandments (Lk 1:6, 50). This phrase has also been translated as "progressing in the faithfulness of the Lord."

The Pentecost of the Gentiles (Acts 10:44–48; 11:15–18)

The conversion of Cornelius and his household is a doctrinal highpoint in the Book of Acts. The event goes beyond the confines of the individual and has repercussions of universal value: The Gentiles are called to the faith.

Luke demonstrates the importance of this fact by the dimensions he gives the story. The account is made up of pieces of different literary genres and, above all, of the appeal to the double vision of Cornelius (10:3–8, 22, 30, 33; 11:13–14) and Peter (10:9–16, 28; 11:5–10). These visions clearly show that the initiative for the admission of the Gentiles to the faith came directly from God, and that Peter humbly and obediently seconded the divine will.

The conversion of the Ethiopian official by Philip was only an individual case (8:26–39). It was in reality Peter who, by the express will of God and under the inspiration of the Holy Spirit, officially opened the doors of the church to the Gentiles (10:19; 11:12).

It would be helpful now to read the whole text (10:1–11:18) in order to fully understand the part on which we wish to place our attention next.

The Double Vision (10:1–33)

One day, about 3:00 pm, the centurion Cornelius had a vision of an angel of God and sent two servants and a soldier to Joppa to fetch Peter (10:1–8). The next day, about midday, Peter fell into a trance (10:9–16). As Peter was reflecting on the vision he was seeing, the Spirit said to him:

> Some men have come to see you. Hurry down, and do not hesitate about going back with them; it was I who told them to come. (10:19–20)

The following day Peter left Caesarea with six brothers, the soldier, and the two servants. After a day's journey Peter entered

Caesarea, where Cornelius was waiting with his relatives and close friends. Cornelius and Peter both told their visions (10:24–32). Then Cornelius added, "Here we all are, assembled in front of you to hear what message God has given you for us" (10:33b).

Testimony of Peter (20:34b–43)

Peter speaks at the invitation of Cornelius. Once again, Peter bears witness to Jesus in the inspiration of the Spirit, who had ordered him to go to the centurion's house (see 10:19; 11:12). This testimony is made up of three parts: an introduction (10:34b–35), a Christological synthesis (10:36–42), and a conclusion (10:43).

Introduction. From Peter's experience comes a principle of universal value for the salvation of all men of all times:

> The truth I have now come to realize ... is that God does not have favorites, but that anybody of any nationality who fears God and does what is right is acceptable to him. (10:34b–35)

In God there is no distinction of persons (Rom 2:10–11; Col 3:25; 1 Pt 1:17). Man is made acceptable to God by his moral conduct and not by the sacrifice of animals (Prv 11:20; 15:8). Furthermore, the prophets Isaiah and Malachi had announced that in messianic times the worship of the Gentiles would be pleasing to God (Is 56:7; Mal 1:10, 11; see Rom 15:16; Phil 4:18; 1 Pt 2:5).

Christological Synthesis. Peter presents a resume of the gospel story, emphasizing the basic elements of the primitive *kerygma:*

1. Jesus the Messiah, the Lord of all, has been sent by God to the sons of Israel as a prophet to announce the good news of peace (Is 52:7).

2. God anointed Jesus of Nazareth with the Holy Spirit and with power. He went about doing good and healing all those oppressed by the devil, because God was with him. Peter and his companions, the Twelve, are witnesses to all that Jesus did in Galilee, Judaea, and Jerusalem. The Apostles are qualified witnesses to Jesus the Messiah (1:8, 22).

3. The Jews killed Jesus, hanging him on a tree.
4. God raised Jesus up the third day.
5. God allowed Jesus to show himself to witnesses the Father had chosen beforehand, not to all the people. They ate and drank with him after he had risen from the dead.
6. Jesus commanded his disciples to preach to the people, and they bore witness that "God has appointed him to judge everyone, alive or dead" (10:42).

Conclusion. Peter's testimony ends with a fundamental principle:

> It is to him that all the prophets bear this witness: that all who believe in Jesus will have their sins forgiven through his name.

Jesus and his work have been announced by God through the prophets. The forgiveness of sins is obtained through faith in the name of Jesus. In Jesus the Messiah, who has died and is risen, made Judge and Lord of all, is salvation for all men, whether Jew or pagan. The indispensable condition for salvation is a lively and working faith, which is also a gift from God.

Outpouring of the Spirit (10:44–48)

> While Peter was still speaking the Holy Spirit came down on all the listeners. Jewish believers who had accompanied Peter were all astonished that the gift of the Holy Spirit should be poured out on the pagans too, since they could hear them speaking strange languages and proclaiming the greatness of God. Peter himself then said, "Could anyone refuse the water of baptism to these people, now they have received the Holy Spirit just as much as we have?" He then gave orders for them to be baptized in the name of Jesus Christ.

Before Peter could finish his teaching—or, perhaps, having only just begun it (11:15)—and without having performed the laying on of hands (8:17), "the Holy Spirit came down on all the listeners." This indicates that the free gift of the Spirit depends more on the divine initiative than on human collaboration. Nevertheless, the proclamation of the word is ordained by God and fills a necessary function (10:20–22:33).

The Holy Spirit is God's gift par excellence (2:38; 8:20; 11:17; Lk 11:9). The expression "came down" indicates an event that is sudden and unexpected (see 2:2). To "be poured out" is an image that comes from the prophet Joel and has passed into the language of the New Testament (Jl 3:1–2; Acts 2:17–18, 33; Rom 5:5; Ti 3:6).

The Spirit makes his presence visible by means of charismatic phenomena. Speaking in tongues and proclaiming the greatness of God, or better, proclaiming the greatness of God in tongues, relates the event at Caesarea with the happening on Pentecost (2:4, 11, 17). This celebration of God in tongues is a working of the prophetic Spirit (see Lk 1:41–42; 1:67; 2:27–32).

Peter instantly understands the profound significance of what happened. Cornelius and his household have received the Holy Spirit like the Twelve on Pentecost. This gift of the spirit has followed interior conversion (11:18) and faith in the Lord Messiah (11:17). God had done his complete work in them: conversion, faith in Jesus, gift of the Spirit (see 2:38). All that was lacking was the tangible sign that would outwardly manifest what had been done in them interiorly. Therefore Peter asks:

> Could anyone refuse the water of baptism to these people, now they have received the Holy Spirit just as much as we have? (10:47)

"He then gave orders for them to be baptized in the name of Jesus Christ" (10:48). Various New Testament texts show us that the Apostles did not ordinarily administer baptism themselves (8:12, 36; 19:5; 1 Cor 1:14, 17). Perhaps in this they are following the example of Jesus (Jn 4:2). "Afterward they begged him to stay on for some days" (10:48b).

> The community of life and, no doubt, of the table, which brings hospitality with it, consecrates the existence of the new church of Caesarea.*

---

*Ibid., p. 391.

Peter in Jerusalem (11:1–18)

Upon learning what had taken place at Caesarea and of Peter's sojourn in a household of Gentiles, the circumcised brethren reproached Peter for having been visiting the uncircumcised and eating with them (11:3). Without explaining his actions in regard to the pagans, Peter recounted at length all that had happened (11:4–14). He then added:

> I had scarcely begun to speak when the Holy Spirit came down on them in the same way as it came on us at the beginning, and I remembered that the Lord had said, "John baptized with water, but you will be baptized with the Holy Spirit." I realized then that God was giving them the identical thing he gave to us when we believed in the Lord Jesus Christ; and who was I to stand in God's way? (11:15–17)

Jesus continued fulfilling his promise, continued baptizing in the Holy Spirit (1:5).

> This account satisfied them, and they gave glory to God. "God" they said "can evidently grant even the pagans the repentance that leads to life." (11:18)

It is interesting to note the elements of Christian initiation present here. They form a strong unity. Luke, more than insisting upon a particular order to the elements, emphasizes the unity and necessity of all of them. Each element contributes its part in making a man a disciple of Christ.

In the first place and above all: the initiative of God. Then: the preaching of the word (19:36–43); conversion (11:18); faith in Jesus–Messiah, Lord and Judge (10:33, 44; 11:17); the outpouring of the Spirit (10:44–47; 11:15–17); the rite of baptism in water (10:47–48; 11:17); the gift of new life (11:18).

The Holy Spirit is the soul of the entire work (10:19, 38, 44–48; 11:12, 15–18). God has the freedom to pour out his Spirit, or to tangibly manifest his presence, before or after the external rite of baptism in water. The Book of Acts shows the impetuous force of the Spirit opening the way for the gospel. The future belongs to him; the gospel cannot be stopped.

CHAPTER NINE

THE GREAT MISSIONS

The Holy Spirit in the Church of Antioch (Acts 11:24, 28; 13:1-3)

The foundation of the church of Antioch, the first church where Gentile disciples predominated, was a happening of capital importance. It can be placed in the years 38-39. Antioch, on the river Orontes, was the capital of the Roman province of Syria and the third city of the empire after Rome and Alexandria.

Foundation of the Church of Antioch (11:19-26)

Evangelization of the Jews (11:19). After the death of Stephen many of the disciples were scattered (see 8:1). These disciples traveled along the Phoenician coast (Ptolemais, Tyre, Sidon, Beirut), arrived at Cyprus, and then went on to Antioch. They proclaimed the word, but only to the Jews.

Evangelization of the Greeks (11:20-24). There were also some Hellenist Jews from Cyprus who were evangelists (Mnason, in 21:16), from Cyrene (Lucius, in 13:1; Alexander and Rufus, sons of Simon of Cyrene in Mk 15:21), and from Syria (Nicholas of Antioch, in 6:5). Having a broader vision and a wider horizon, they began to address themselves also to the pagans (the "Greeks"), proclaiming to them the good news of the Lord Jesus.

While Jesus was preached to the Jews as "Messiah," he was announced to the Gentiles as "Lord." For the latter, the title "messiah" meant very little, while the title "Lord" was full of meaning. The emperor of Rome was called "the Lord" and was recognized as having a unique, regal power, absolute and universal, almost divine (25:26). Therefore, in announcing Jesus as the Lord, the disciples were communicating their faith in Jesus to the Gentiles, not only as Lord of an empire, but as the one exalted at the right hand of God and made sovereign of the kingdom to come (see 2:21, 36; 7:59–60; 10:36; 1 Thes 4:15–17; 2 Thes 1:7–12; Rom 10:9–13).

The mission to Antioch was crowned with surprising success: Many embraced the faith and were converted to the Lord. The hand of the Lord was with them. God assisted the evangelistic initiative of the Hellenists with his power and protection.

The news of the conversion of the pagans eventually arrived at the mother church in Jerusalem. This church enjoyed a natural preeminence and exercised certain rights of supervision with respect to the other churches (see 8:14; 9:32; 11:1; Gal 2:2). Having received the good news of the foundation at Antioch, the brethren in Jerusalem decided it would be opportune to send the new church a delegation. Who should they send? They chose Barnabas, a man like Stephen, "a good man, filled with the Holy Spirit and with faith" (Acts 11:24).

The mention of the Holy Spirit is significant. Through Barnabas the Holy Spirit would effectively motivate the evangelization of the pagans. In fact, "there he could see for himself that God had given grace, and this pleased him, and he urged them all to remain faithful to the Lord with heartfelt devotion" (11:23). A considerable multitude was converted to the Lord.

Saul in Antioch (11:25–26a). Once established in Antioch Barnabas set out for Tarsus to look for Saul. Having found him, he brought him to Antioch, where they remained together a year teaching the community.

The "Christians" (11:26b). At Antioch the disciples were called Christians for the first time. The Gentiles probably gave this name to the followers of Jesus as a nickname. "Messiah" in Greek means "Christ."

The appearance of this title in Antioch makes one think that the new religion did not appear there simply as a Jewish sect, but as an independent religious group that stemmed from Christ (see 26:28; 1 Pt 4:16).

Agabus, Prophet of the Spirit (11:27–30)

> While they were there some prophets came down to Antioch from Jerusalem, and one of them whose name was Agabus, seized by the Spirit, stood up and predicted that a famine would spread over the whole empire. This in fact happened before the reign of Claudius came to an end. (11:27–28)

This passage tells us that there were prophets in the church of Jerusalem (as was also true in the church of Antioch [13:1]). The prophetic charism will appear in Ephesus (19:6) and in Caesarea (21:9ff) as well. The prophets fill various functions, among them the foretelling of certain events affecting the life of the Christian communities (11:28; 21:10–14).

Enlightened by the Spirit, Agabus prophesies that a great famine will come upon the Roman empire. This famine did in fact take place between A.D. 46 and 48. The church of Antioch, conscious of her communion with the churches of Judaea, wants to express her active, fraternal love by sending help. Barnabas and Saul were commissioned to bring this help to Jerusalem.

Barnabas and Saul, Missionaries of the Spirit (13:1–3)

The church of Antioch was presided over by five people: Barnabas, Simeon Niger, Lucius of Cyrene, Manaen, and Saul. All five were Hellenist Jews. Barnabas was probably the leader, by virtue of his position as delegate of the church in Jerusalem (11:22). Saul is named last because he is the last to arrive (11:25–26). The elders have received charisms from the Holy Spirit; they were prophets and teachers.

The charism of prophecy in the New Testament. Like the prophets of the Old Testament, those of the New Testament are charismatic men and women who speak in the name of God at the inspiration of the Holy Spirit (see Dt 18:18; 2 Pt 1:21; Mt 5:12; 1 Cor 12:10). Under the New Covenant there is a fuller outpouring of this charism, and all the faithful benefit from it (2:17–18; 19:6; 1 Cor 11:4–5; 14:26, 29–33, 37). However, some people are especially gifted with this charism, to the point of meriting the title "prophets" (11:27; 13:1; 15:32; 21:9–10).

In the hierarchy of charisms the prophets normally come in second place, after the apostles (1 Cor 12:28–29; Eph 4:11; but see 1 Cor 12:10; Rom 12:6; Lk 11:49). It is they who are the accredited witnesses of the Spirit (1 Thes 5:19–20; Rv 1:3; 2:7), who pass on his revelations (1 Cor 14:6, 26, 30; Eph 3:5; Rv 1:1), whereas the apostles are the witnesses of the risen Christ (Rom 1:1; Acts 1:8), who announce the *kerygma* (2:22).

The function of the prophets is not limited to predicting the future (11:28; 21:11) or to reading hearts (1 Cor 14:24–25; see 1 Tm 1:18; 4:14). If they build up, exhort, and console (1 Cor 14:3; see Acts 4:36; 11:23–24), it is due to the revelations of the Spirit which they receive. These revelations are similar to tongues (2:4; 19:6), but are ranked ahead of tongues because they are intelligible (1 Cor 14).

The principal role of the prophets appears to have been that of explaining, by the light of the Holy Spirit, the prophecies of scripture (1 Pt 1:10–12) and, consequently, uncovering the mystery of the divine plan (1 Cor 13:2; Eph 3:5; Rom 16:25). Therefore they are associated with apostles in their role as pillars of the church (Eph 2:20).

The Book of Revelation is a typical example of prophecy in the New Testament (Rv 1:3; 10:11; 19:10; 22:7–10, 18–19). The charism of prophecy, however elevated it may be, does not give more than an imperfect and provisional understanding, linked as it is to faith (Rom 12:6), which will disappear in the face of the beatific vision (1 Cor 13:8–12).

The charism of didascalia or teaching. The charism proper to a teacher gives a person the ability to expound a moral or doctrinal teaching, normally based on scripture (1 Cor 12:14). Paul intimately links the two charisms of prophecy and teaching (1 Cor 14:6,26). In 1 Cor 12:28–29 the teachers are listed as third in importance, after the apostles and prophets. In Eph 4:11 the teachers and pastors appear to form a single category.

The five prophets and teachers who preside over the church of Antioch make up a group which ought to be seen in relation to the group of the Twelve (1:13) and the group of the Seven (6:5). The group of the Five were Hellenist Jews.

One of the prophets in Antioch must have given the message cited by Luke in the following passage:

> One day while they were offering worship to the Lord and keeping a fast, the Holy Spirit said, "I want Barnabas and Saul set apart for the work to which I have called them." (13:2)

In the Septuagint the Greek verb *leiturgeo* denotes the Temple worship offered to Yahweh in Jerusalem (2 Chr 13:10; Heb 10:11; Rom 15:16). In Christian assemblies the ancient worship of the Chosen People has been replaced by the new: prayers, songs, and the breaking of the bread. In this liturgy the Lord Jesus has a central place. At the moment of the calling of Saul and Barnabas it is likely that the community at Antioch was celebrating the Eucharist (20:7).

The word of the Spirit concerning Barnabas and Saul is important: It highlights the "call" which God gives to his servants so that they may fulfill a mission for him. It should be noted that the initiative comes from God and, here specifically, from the Holy Spirit.

Various strands make up the vocation of Barnabas and Saul. By weaving these elements together we arrive at a descriptive definition of vocation: a free and permanent supernatural gift from the Holy Spirit, which sets a person apart for God with the end of entrusting him with a work to carry out.

> So it was that after fasting and prayer they laid their hands on them and sent them off. (13:3)

Fasting and prayer go together. Christians have inherited this practice from Judaism (Ezr 8:21–23; Neh 1:4; Tb 12:8; Lk 2:37; 5:33; Acts 14:23). The laying on of hands on this occasion does not signify that the community is investing Barnabas and Saul with additional authority, since they were already the leaders of the local church, and the one who now calls and chooses them is the Holy Spirit directly. The laying on of hands here is a gesture through which the assembly commends those called by the Holy Spirit to the grace of God (see 14:26).

In this passage Barnabas comes before Saul. As the one sent out by the church in Jerusalem it appears that he is the head of the mission (see 4:36; 9:27; 11:22–30).

The Holy Spirit, Soul of the Missions (Acts 13:4, 9, 52)

"You will be my witnesses ... to the ends of the earth" were Jesus' words (1:8). Luke will now depict a further phase in the expansion of Christianity. The gospel grows and spreads, overflowing the frontiers of Syria and arriving in the fully Hellenist world of the Roman provinces of Pamphylia, Pisidia, and Iconium. This mission could well have taken place during the years 45–49. The soul of the whole mission is the Holy Spirit.

Barnabas and Saul, "sent on their mission by the Holy Spirit, went down to Seleucia and from there sailed to Cyprus" (13:4). The new apostles leave Antioch. In spite of her bad reputation as a great pagan city, Antioch was becoming a missionary center of prime importance (13:1–3; 14:26–28; 15:35–36; 18:22).

The Greek verb used by Luke for the sending out of the apostles is very expressive: *ekpempo*. This word has the connotation of "being launched," communicating very effectively the vigor and forcefulness of their starting out. Barnabas and Saul are sent by the Holy Spirit. The Holy Spirit called them and set them apart for himself with the object of fulfilling a work. They are, therefore, his missionaries.

Upon their arrival in Salamis, the eastern door of the island, they set out right away to announce the word of God to the Jews. Throughout his apostolic career Saul will always observe the custom of first preaching the good news to his brothers in race and religion. Luke emphasizes this throughout Acts (13:14; 14:1; 16:13; 17:2, 10, 17; 18:4, 19; 19:8; 28:17, 23). Saul's practice is in accord with a theological principle: A special priority in the proclamation of the word of God belongs to the Jews (3:26; 13:46; Rom 1:16; 2:9–10; Mk 7:27). Only after the Jews reject the message does Paul turn to the Gentiles (13:46; 18:6; 28:28).

The apostles traveled across the island and arrived at Paphos. There the proconsul Sergius Paulus called for Barnabas and Saul to appear before him. He was a prudent man and eager to hear the word of God. But a false Jewish prophet, the magician Bar-jesus or Elymas Magos, tried to hinder the proconsul from receiving the faith. Filled with the Spirit, Saul

> looked him full in the face and said, "You utter fraud, you imposter, you son of the devil, you enemy of all true religion, why don't you stop twisting the straightforward ways of the Lord? Now watch how the hand of the Lord will strike you: you will be blind, and for a time you will not see the sun." (13:9–10)

Instantly darkness fell upon him, and he walked around looking for someone to take him by the hand. Seeing what had happened, the proconsul believed, amazed by the teaching of the Lord.

The blindness with which Elymas was punished is a sign which carries a double message: It exposes the deception and evil of the magician, and manifests the truth of the word of God proclaimed by Barnabas and Saul, who are instruments filled with the Holy Spirit.

The Holy Spirit, who had launched the apostles Barnabas and Saul from Antioch, continually accompanied them with his power in the preaching of the faith. He manifested his power through them, mowing down obstacles that would oppose the gospel.

On the occasion of the conversion of the Roman proconsul, Luke mentions Saul's Roman name—Paul—for the first time. It is by his Roman name that Paul will be called in the rest of Acts. As the Jews had a custom of having a double name, it is likely that Saul had had this name before. Nevertheless, what should be noted is that Luke intentionally reveals the Roman name of Paul at the moment when the imperial proconsul embraces the faith. Furthermore, from this time on Paul passes to the center of the stage and appears to become the head of the mission (see 13:13).

From Paphos, Paul and his companions took ship for Atalia and arrived at Perga. John returned to Jerusalem, while the others continued on to Antioch in Pisidia. On the sabbath they went to the synagogue. Following the reading of the Law and the Prophets, Paul stood up and delivered an important discourse (13:16b-41). Many Jews and Gentiles who feared and worshiped God followed Paul and Barnabas, and the apostles persuaded them to persevere in God's grace—the free gift of faith.

Paul and Barnabas preached also to the Gentiles, or at least to those aware of what had happened. The following sabbath "almost the whole town assembled to hear the word of God" (13:44). This made the Jews envious. They rebelled against the apostles, and Paul and Barnabas left the Jews and turned to the Gentiles. At this, Paul cited a portion of Is 49:6: "I have made you a light for the nations, so that my salvation may reach the ends of the earth" (Acts 13:47). On hearing Paul the Gentiles rejoiced and began to glorify the Lord for his word. All who were destined for eternal life believed, and the word of the Lord spread throughout the entire region (13:48b-49).

But the Jews stirred up the principal leaders of the city and distinguished women who worshiped God. They incited a persecution of Paul and Barnabas and threw them out of their territory. The two apostles shook off the dust from their feet and left for Iconium. "But the disciples were filled with joy and the Holy Spirit" (13:52).

The Holy Spirit, at whose inspiration the mission had begun (13:4), was fulfilling step by step the work for which he had set Paul and Barnabas apart. Like in Jerusalem, Samaria, Caesarea, and Antioch, here too he was filling the hearts of believers. He fell upon them and was poured out upon them with his gifts, the manifestations of his working presence. And he produced in them the fruit of happiness and joy (see 1 Thes 1:6; Gal 5:22).

"It has been decided by the Holy Spirit and by ourselves..." (Acts 15:8, 27, 29, 32)

Controversy in Antioch (15:1–2; Gal 2:1)

> Then some men came down from Judaea and taught the brothers, "Unless you have yourselves circumcised in the tradition of Moses you cannot be saved." This led to disagreement, and after Paul and Barnabas had had a long argument with these men it was arranged that Paul and Barnabas and others of the church should go up to Jerusalem and discuss the problem with the apostles and elders. (15:1–2)

As one can see, the problem under discussion was of transcendent importance and touched upon fundamental principles of the faith. The Jewish Christians were insisting upon circumcision and, consequently, the observance of the Law of Moses as a requirement for obtaining salvation (15:5). They were saying, in other words, that to attain the salvation made available by Jesus it is necessary to first embrace Judaism.

Paul and Barnabas did not agree with that. They were convinced that salvation is attained not by observance of the Law, but only through faith in the Lord Jesus (15:11; Gal 2:15–20; 3:10–12).

Things being as they were, the church at Antioch decided to send Paul and Barnabas to Jerusalem so that they could discuss the matter with the Apostles and elders. Others accompanied them, among them Titus, a Greek who had become a Christian without ascribing to the observances of the Law (Gal 2:1).

The Meeting with the Leaders in Jerusalem (15:3–12; Gal 2:1–10)

> As they passed through Phoenicia and Samaria they told how the pagans had been converted, and this news was received with the greatest satisfaction by the brothers. When they arrived in Jerusalem they were welcomed by the church and by the apostles and elders, and gave an account of all that God had done with them. (15:3–4)

Then, in a private conference with the elders, Paul explained the gospel he was preaching among the Gentiles, with the object of knowing whether or not his efforts had been in vain. This group of elders, Paul tells us, was made up of James, Cephas, and John (Gal 2:9).

After the meeting we see that not even Titus, Paul's Greek companion, was obliged to be circumcised. This means that the authorities of the mother church in Jerusalem agreed with the teaching of Paul and Barnabas. In order to be saved, neither circumcision nor observance of the Mosaic Law is necessary, only faith in the Lord Jesus.

Controversy with false brethren. But then, in a public meeting a serious discussion was stirred up by some Pharisee converts to Christianity, whom Paul called false brethren. These Pharisees insisted "that the pagans should be circumcised and instructed to keep the Law of Moses" (15:5).

Peter's decision. The Apostles and elders met together in order to deal with the matter. After a long discussion Peter stood up and said:

> My brothers ... you know perfectly well that in the early days God made his choice among you: the pagans were to learn the good news from me and so become believers. In fact God, who can read everyone's heart, showed his approval of them by giving the Holy Spirit to them just as he had to us. God made no distinction between them and us, since he purified their hearts by faith. It would only provoke God's anger now, surely, if you imposed on the disciples the very burden that neither we nor our ancestors were strong enough to support. Remember, we believe that we are saved in the same way as they are: through the grace of the Lord Jesus. (15:6–12)

Peter is clearly referring to the admission of Cornelius and his household of faith (10:1–11, 18). The present decision of the Apostle is a consequence of the personal experience given him by the Holy Spirit (10:19, 44–48; 11:12, 15, 17).

To require converted Gentiles to observe the Law would be to tempt God—it would be tantamount to demanding miraculous signs of his will when God had already expressed his will by sending the gift of the Holy Spirit to Cornelius and his house. To fail to deduce the obvious consequences of God's action would be to demand that God intervene again, which would betray a blasphemous attitude.

> This silenced the entire assembly, and they listened to Barnabas and Paul describing all the signs and wonders God had worked through them among the pagans. (15:12)

Intervention of James, and the Apostolic Letter (15:13-19)

After Peter's decision the Book of Acts presents a speech given by James. James touches upon a point outside the question of circumcision and observance of the Law: the rules of fellowship. This was an area of practical and pastoral concern, brought up in order to promote harmony between Jewish Christians and pagan converts.

How should Christians coming from Gentile backgrounds act in regard to certain things which profoundly shock the mentality and traditions of Christians coming from Judaism? For ages the Jews had been accustomed to hear certain prescriptions enjoined upon them in the synagogues each sabbath. Nonobservance of these rules would cause deep suffering to the traditional religious psychology of the Jews. Therefore, James concludes:

> I rule, then, that instead of making things more difficult for pagans who turn to God, we send them a letter telling them merely to abstain from anything polluted by idols, from fornication, from the meat of strangled animals and from blood. (15:20)

In agreement with these decisions the Apostles and elders, together with the whole church, selected two representatives from the mother church—Judas Barsabbas and Silas. They accompanied Paul and Barnabas to Antioch with an official letter and an oral message for the churches of Antioch, Syria, and Cilicia. Here is the letter:

The apostles and elders, your brothers, send greetings to the brothers of pagan birth in Antioch, Syria, and Cilicia. We hear that some of our members have disturbed you with their demands and have unsettled your minds. They acted without any authority from us, and so we have decided unanimously to elect delegates and to send them to you with Barnabas and Paul, men we highly respect who have dedicated their lives to the name of our Lord Jesus Christ. Accordingly we are sending you Judas and Silas, who will confirm by word of mouth what we have written in this letter. It has been decided by the Holy Spirit and by ourselves not to saddle you with any burden beyond these essentials: you are to abstain from food sacrificed to idols, from blood, from the meat of strangled animals and from fornication. Avoid these, and you will do what is right. Farewell. (15:23–29)

The Western Text adds an expression very much in line with the theology of the Spirit Luke is expounding. In verse 29 we read, "Avoid these, and you will do what is right under the guidance of the Holy Spirit. Farewell." The faithful will be able to keep the guidlines of the assembly, since they will be under the guidance of the Holy Spirit.

It is good to emphasize here that this ecclesiastical decision was the work of the Holy Spirit and the legitimate authority together: "It has been decided by the Holy Spirit and by ourselves" (15:28). The Holy Spirit is the one who inspired the decision made by the assembly in Jerusalem.

The Delegation in Antioch (15:30–35)

The delegates of the council—Judas, Silas, Barnabas, and Paul—went down to Antioch, gathered the assembly, and delivered the letter. The community read it and rejoiced upon receiving that encouragement.

After some time, the delegation was sent off in peace to return to those who had sent them, but Silas decided to remain. As for Paul and Barnabas, "they stayed on in Antioch, and there with many others they taught and proclaimed the good news, the word of the Lord" (15:35).

Obedient to the Guidance of the Spirit (Acts 16:6–7)

On recounting the second missionary journey of Paul, Luke does not try to relate in exact detail all that the Apostle did. Instead, by means of several representative stories, he tells how the gospel spread to Europe and arrived in the heart of Greece (15:36–18:22).

After spending some days in Antioch Paul took Silas for a companion and departed, commended to the grace of God by the brothers. The missionaries traveled through Syria and Cilicia, strengthening the churches in their faith. They visited Derbe and Lystra. Paul came to know Timothy in Lystra and wanted him to join them.

The author of Acts tells us that the churches were growing in numbers from day to day. Then he affirms that the itinerary of the missionaries was guided by the Spirit. "They traveled through Phrygia and the Galatian country, having been told by the Holy Spirit not to preach the word in Asia" (16:6).

On leaving Iconium Paul wanted to head toward the Roman province of Asia, especially to Ephesus, the capital, but he was impeded by the Holy Spirit. So, after traveling across Phrygia, he took the road north to Galatian territory.

> When they reached the frontier of Mysia they thought to cross it into Bithynia, but as the Spirit of Jesus would not allow them, they went through Mysia and came down to Troas. (16:7)

The apostles wanted to continue northward to Bithynia, probably to the cities of Nicea and Nicomedia, but for the second time the Spirit did not allow it.

The gospel is the good news of Jesus. Because the Holy Spirit is the guiding force in the work of evangelization, the role of Jesus and the role of the Spirit are closely intertwined here. Luke makes this clear by refering the the Spirit as the "Spirit of Jesus."

Luke does not inform us of the way in which the Holy Spirit manifested his will on those occasions when he re-routed Paul and Silas; it could have been through revelation or simply through the circumstances of life. What is important to Luke is to show that the work of evangelization depends more on the will of the Holy Spirit, who guides and directs the missionaries, than on the missionaries themselves. Later, Paul will remind the Galatians that the occasion of preaching the gospel to them was a sickness with which he had been afflicted (Gal 4:12ff).

The Outpouring of the Spirit in Ephesus (Acts 19:1-7)

Paul later traveled to Phrygia. The Western Text presents an interesting variation on 19:1. In place of the phrase "While Apollos was in Corinth" it gives:

> When Paul, pursuing his own plan, wanted to set out for Jerusalem, the Spirit told him to go back to Asia.

Once again Paul shows himself receptive to the movement of the Spirit and disposed to follow his inspiration immediately. And again, the mission of evangelization is shown to be the enterprise of the Spirit.

After passing through some mountainous regions Paul arrived at Ephesus.

> Ephesus, with Alexandria, was then one of the most beautiful cities of the empire. A great religious, political, and commercial center, it had a mixed population, amounting to more or less three hundred thousand inhabitants. Even though it was the captital of proconsular Asia, it enjoyed a certain autonomy under the high control of the proconsul.*

In Ephesus Paul found some disciples and asked them, "Did you receive the Holy Spirit when you became believers?" (19:2a). The word "disciples" is used to designate "Christians" (6:1, 27; 9:1, 10, 19, 25, 26, 38; etc). Paul must have noticed the lack of certain Christian characteristics in those disciples, and among them the tangible, charismatic manifestations that attest to the presence of the Spirit (see 2:1-4; 8:14-19; 10:46).

**La Biblia de Jerusalén*, p. 1580.

To Paul's question the disciples responded, "No, we were never even told there was such a thing as a Holy Spirit" (19:2b). How should we understand this answer? It probably does not mean that they were ignorant of the very existence of the Spirit of God, for this would be inconceivable in believing disciples who have received even a minimal understanding of scripture. More likely, it refers to the charismatic gift of the Holy Spirit as fulfillment of the messianic prophecies (2:17–18, 33; Jn 7:39).

Paul persisted, "Then how were you baptized?" They replied, "With John's baptism." Then Paul said:

> John's baptism ... was a baptism of repentance; but he insisted that the people should believe in the one who was to come after him—in other words, Jesus. (19:3–4)

The disciples must have accepted the teachings the Apostle gave them.

> When they heard this, they were baptized in the name of the Lord Jesus, and the momemt Paul had laid hands on them the Holy Spirit came down on them, and they began to speak with tongues and to prophesy. (19:5–6)

On accepting the faith, those disciples were baptized. Christian baptism in the name of Jesus (2:38) here appears distinctly different from John's baptism, which was baptism in water for conversion.

Even more, Christian or messianic baptism is a baptism in the Holy Spirit (1:5). Therefore, the outpouring of the Spirit follows immediately upon baptism in water. This outpouring takes place at the imposition of hands by an Apostle. Once again, baptism in the name of Jesus, the Messiah, and the gift of the Holy Spirit are closely linked (see 2:38, 8:14–17; 9:17–18; 10:47–48; 11:15–17).

The disciples did not have to wait a long time to experience tangible charismatic manifestations: "And they began to speak with tongues and to prophesy" (19:6). This description recalls what happened to Cornelius and his household in Caesarea (10:46).

It is interesting to note that the evangelization of Ephesus, a city which will play a very important role in the history of the development of the Christian faith, begins with a great outpouring of the Holy Spirit. Luke wants to show through this the spiritual nature of the establishment of Christianity in this major Greco-Roman commercial and religious center. Perhaps this is also the reason for revealing the number of those new disciples, which was a number full of symbolism. "There were about twelve of these men" (19:7).

Ephesus, with its twelve disciples who had not yet received the Holy Spirit, was like another Jerusalem, whose twelve disciples had been in an upper room awaiting the promise of the Father (see 2:13).

Indeed, we notice that Luke, in describing the progress of evangelization, has sought to emphasize special outpourings of the Holy Spirit: in Jerusalem, at the birth of the church (2:1–41); in Samaria, when the Samaritans, adherents of an unenlightened religion, open up to faith in Christ (8:5–25); in Paul, when the great Apostle of the Gentiles is baptized (9:1–19a); in Caesarea, when the pagans are admitted to the faith (10:1–11, 18); in Ephesus, when the spiritual conquest of the Greek world for the Lord Jesus begins (19:1–7).

The Holy Spirit in Paul's Discourse at Miletus (Acts 20:23,28)

At the end of his third missionary journey Paul decided to go to Jerusalem to bring alms to the brothers and sisters there (2 Cor 8–9). He left Greece, passed through Macedonia, and embarked for Troas from Philippi (Neapolis). From Troas, a whole group went with him through Assos, Mitylene, Chios, Samos, and Trogyllium until arriving at Miletus. Paul did not want to lose time by going through Ephesus, since he wanted to be in Jerusalem for Pentecost (20:16). Therefore, when he arrived at Miletus he sent for the elders of the community in Ephesus (see 20:3–17).

Luke records a long speech by Paul which was directed to the elders of that important church Paul had founded (20:18–35). This speech is actually a farewell discourse, a pastoral "last testament" of the Apostle: It recalls the responsibilities of the ministry, the demands of apostolic service, and the power of the divine grace upon which all depends.

The discourse has considerable doctrinal richness. It touches upon various themes of Lucan and Pauline theology: service to the Lord, the testimony of the gospel, conversion, faith, suffering for Jesus, the kingdom, the action of the Spirit on behalf of the church of God, redemption by the blood of Jesus, enemies of the faith, the work of the grace of God, the inheritance of the saints, personal work, teaching, and charity to the poor. Of particular note is the Trinitarian base of the discourse, throughout which are interwoven references to God the Father (20:24, 27, 28, 32), the Lord Jesus (20:19, 21, 24, 25), and the Holy Spirit (20:22, 23–28).

> And now you see me a prisoner already in Spirit; I am on my way to Jerusalem, but have no idea what will happen to me there, except that the Holy Spirit, in town after town, has made it clear enough that imprisonment and persecution await me. But life to me is not a thing to waste words on, provided that when I finish my race I have carried out the mission the Lord Jesus gave me—and that was to bear witness to the good news of God's grace. (20:22–24)

Even before leaving Corinth, Paul had felt very uneasy about what might be awaiting him in Jerusalem (Rom 15:30–31). Now in Miletus his forebodings become more explicit, but he knows that his whole life is guided and directed by the Holy Spirit. He is an instrument of the Spirit for the sake of the gospel. If imprisonment awaits him, this will depend more on the will of the Spirit than on the schemes of his enemies. Through his prophetic word the Spirit himself is preparing Paul for his next painful destination.

> Be on your guard for yourselves and for all the flock of which the Holy Spirit has made you the overseers, to feed the church of God which he bought with his own blood. (20:28)

The charisms come from the Holy Spirit to build up the church (1 Cor 12:7, 11). It is the Spirit who has placed the elders of Ephesus as *episcopoi,* that is, as guardians and overseers. They should pastor the church of God as one would pastor a flock. The term *episcopoi* (singular, *episcopos*) here denotes a function that the elders discharge in the community (Phil 1:1; Ti 1:5–7; 1 Tm 3:1–6). Only later will the president of the college of elders become a monarchical bishop responsible for a local church.

The metaphor of the flock was applied in the Old Testament to the people of Israel (Ez 34; Is 40:11; 49:9–10). In the Gospels the "little flock" is made up of the disciples of Jesus (Lk 12:32; Mk 14:27; Jn 10:1–16, 27; 21:15–17). In the Book of Acts the flock is the church of God (see 1 Pt 5:1–3).

> As used here this expression certainly refers to the local church of Ephesus, but the solemnity of the context invites one to think that, for this last use of the word "church" in Acts, this restricted meaning opens up to a fuller sense: the church, the people of God all together (see Eph 1:14; 5:25–27).*

The Christian church has been a costly acquisition: It has required the blood of the Son of God. The original Greek text is extremely compact: "... to pastor the church of God which he acquired with his own blood." As "blood" cannot refer to God the Father, one must understand it as referring to Jesus. Thus the focus of the phrase goes from the Father of the Son (see 1 Pt 1:18–19; Eph 5:25–27; Heb 9:12–14; 13:12).

The Holy Spirit Predicts Paul's Captivity (Acts 21:4, 11)

Continuing his journey toward Jerusalem, Paul and his companions left Miletus. Next they touched Cos, Rhodes, and Patara, bypassed Cyprus, and continued until they reached Tyre (21:1–3).

They stayed in Tyre seven days. The disciples, "speaking in the Spirit," told Paul not to go up to Jerusalem (21:4). "These prophets

---
*La traduction oecuménique de la Bible, p. 420.

did not give Paul an order, but rather, enlightened by the Spirit as to the fate awaiting him, they wished him, out of the love they had for him, to avoid such a fate."*

Resuming their journey, they left Tyre and went to Ptolemais, where they greeted the brothers. The next day they arrived at Caesarea and lodged in the house of Philip the Evangelist. They stayed there several days. Philip had four virgin daughters who were prophets (21:7-9).

While in Caesarea the prophet Agabus came down from Judaea and performed a symbolic, prophetic action for Paul in the style of the ancient prophets (Is 20; Jer 13:1-14; 19:1-3; 1 Kgs 22:11). He took Paul's belt, tied Paul's hands and feet, and said:

> This is what the Holy Spirit says, "The man this girdle belongs to will be bound like this by the Jews in Jerusalem, and handed over to the pagans." (21:11)

Upon hearing this, everyone begged Paul not to go up to Jerusalem, but he, with heroic resolve, answered:

> What are you trying to do—weaken my resolution by your tears? For my part, I am ready not only to be tied up but even to die in Jerusalem for the name of the Lord Jesus. (21:13)

The others could do no more than answer, "The Lord's will be done!" (21:14).

This pronouncement of Agabus roughly corresponds to the story of Paul's arrest (21:31-33). It also closely resembles the account of the passion of Jesus (Lk 18:31-34; see Phil 3:10; Col 1:24).

The Holy Spirit was again revealing, step by step, the fate awaiting Paul in Jerusalem, which would be a prelude to his long imprisonment in Caesarea and Rome. The captivity of the Apostle will not only be the natural consequence of the events which take place, but a mysterious part of the providential plan of God.

---
*La Biblia de Jerusalén, p. 1584.

The Holy Spirit Spoke Through Isaiah (Acts 28:25)

After two years in prison in Caesarea, Paul appealed to Caesar before the procurator Festus. By this act Festus was obligated to send him to Rome (see 25:1—28:16).

Three days after arriving in Rome, Paul called together the leading Jews of the city and told them why he was there. The reason for his chains, he said, was for having proclaimed "the hope of Israel," namely, the belief that God will raise the dead (28:20).

The Jews answered Paul by saying that they had not received any charge against him, and that they did wish to hear more about this "sect" which was finding condemnation everywhere. They set a date to hear more from him about it.

Paul's talk covered two themes: the kingdom of God, a basic scriptural theme, and the good news of Jesus, based on Moses and the Prophets (28:23).

The meeting was long, from morning until evening and, as usual, the result was partly positive, partly negative. Some believed on account of Paul's words; others remained unbelieving (28:24; see 13:42–47). In the face of the negative reaction, Paul finds one more time that this hardness could exist only because it is part of God's plan, predicted already in a word from the Holy Spirit through the prophet Isaiah:

> Go to this nation and say: You will hear and hear again but not understand, see and see again, but not perceive. For the heart of this nation has grown coarse, their ears are dull of hearing and they have shut their eyes, for fear they should see with their eyes, hear with their ears, understand with their heart, and be converted and be healed by me. (28:26–27; see Is 6:9–10)

This text was very familiar to members of the early church for its role in explaining the mystery of the Jews' rejection of Jesus, the Messiah sent by God (see Mk 4:12; Mt 13:14–15; Lk 8:10; Jn 12:40). Isaiah's prophecy finds a fulfillment in the attitude of the Jews. The rejection of the gospel by the majority of the Chosen

People is seen as one of the events foretold by the Holy Spirit, and so remains part of the saving plan of God.

Paul adds, "Understand then, that this salvation of God has been sent to the pagans; they will listen to it" (28:28). Luke ends the Acts of the Apostles with this solemn declaration. These words, firm and incisive, appear to suggest that in those moments a particular program of evangelization is ending, and a new stage in God's plan is about to begin. The great Gentile world is going to receive, with a wide heart and open spirit, the salvation of God!

The Holy Spirit, the Spirit of Jesus, will continue his work of providing the impulse to missionaries of all time, in order that they may continue bearing witness to Jesus, even to the ends of the earth.

BIBLIOGRAPHY

Gospel of Matthew

Albright, William Foxwell, and Mann, C. S. *Matthew.* In *The Anchor Bible.* Garden City, N.Y.: Doubleday, 1971.

Allen, Willoughby C. *A Critical and Exegetical Commentary on the Gospel according to St. Matthew.* 3rd edition. In *The International Critical Commentary.* Edinburgh: T. & T. Clark, 1957.

Benoît, Pierre. *L'Evangile selon Saint Matthieu.* Paris: Editions du Cerf, 1953.

Benoît, Pierre and Boismard, M. Emile. *Synopose des quatre Evangiles.* Vol. II. Paris: Les Editions du Cerf, 1972.

Bonnard, Pierre. *L'Evangile selon Saint Matthieu.* Neuchatel-Paris: Delachaux and Niestlé, 1963.

Durand, Alfred. *Evangile selon Saint Matthieu.* Paris: Beauchesne, 1963.

Goma Civit, Isidro. *El Evangelio según San Mateo (1–13).* Madrid: Ediciones Marova, 1966.

Lagrange, Marie-Joseph. *Evangile selon Saint Matthieu.* Paris: J. Gabalda, 1923.

Lancellotti, Angelo. *Matteo.* Roma: Edizioni Paoline, 1975.

McNeile, A. Hugh. *The Gospel according to St. Matthew.* London: Macmillan & Co., 1961.

Muñoz Iglesias, Salvador. *El Evangelio de la infancia en San Mateo. Sacra Pagina.* In *Miscellanea Biblica Congressus Internationalis Catholici de Re Biblica.* Vol. II. pp. 121–149. Paris-Gembloux: Gabalda-Duculot, 1959.

Paul, André. *L'Evangile de l'enfance selon Saint Matthieu*. Paris: Les Editions du Cerf, 1968.
Radermakers, Jean. *Au fil de l'Evangile selon Saint Matthieu*. Bruxelles: Institut d'études théologiques, 1974.
Sabourin, Leopold. *Il Vangelo di Matteo. Teologia e Esegesi*. 2 Vols. Roma: Edizioni Paoline, 1976–77.
Trilling, Wolfgang. *Das Evangelium nach Matthäus*. (Geistliche Schriftlesung). Düsseldorf: Patmos-Verlag, 1962.
Troadec, Henri Joseph. *Comentario a los Evangelios sinópticos*. In *Actualidad Bíblica* 17. Madrid: Ediciones Fax, 1972.

Gospel of Mark

Alonso Diaz, José. *Evangelio de San Marcos*. Madrid: Biblioteca de Autores Cristianos, 1964.
Cranfield, C. E. B. *The Gospel according to St. Mark*. Cambridge: University Press, 1963.
Gould, Ezra Palmer. *A Critical and Exegetical Commentary on the Gospel according to St. Mark*. In *The International Critical Commentary*. Edinburgh: T. & T. Clark, 1961.
Huby, Joseph. *Evangelio según San Marcos*. Madrid: Ediciones Paulinas, 1963.
Lagrange, Marie-Joseph. *Evangile selon Saint Marc*. Paris: J. Gabalda, 1920.
Schmid, Josef. *El Evangelio según San Marcos*. Barcelona: Herder, 1967.
Schnackenburg, Rudolf. *Das Evangelium nach Markus*. In *Geistliche Schriftlesung*. Düsseldorf: Patmos-Verlag, 1971.
Taylor, Vincent. *The Gospel according to St. Mark*. New York: St. Martin's Press, 1959.

Gospel of Luke

Ellis, E. Earle. *The Gospel of Luke*. London-Edinburgh: Thomas Nelson, 1966.
Lagrange, Marie-Joseph. *Evangile selon Saint Luc*. Paris: J. Gabalda, 1921.
Laurentin, René. *Structure et théologie de Luc*. Vols. I-II. Paris: J. Gabalda, 1957.

Leal, Juan. *Evangelio según San Lucas.* In *La Sagrada Escritura Nuevo Testamento.* Vol. I. Madrid: Biblioteca de Autores Cristianos, 1961.

Osty, E. *L'Evangile selon Saint Luc.* Paris: J. Gabalda, 1921.

Plummer, Alfred. *A Critical and Exegetical Commentary on the Gospel according to St. Luke.* 5th ed. In *The International Critical Commentary.* Edinburgh: T. & T. Clark, 1960.

Schmid, Josef. *El Evangelio según San Lucas.* Barcelona: Herder, 1968.

Stoger, Alois. *Das Evangelium nach Lukas.* In *Geistliche Schriftlesung.* Düsseldorf: Patmos-Verlag, 1963.

Stuhlmueller, Carroll. *The Gospel according to Luke.* In *The Jerome Biblical Commentary.* Vol. II. pp. 115–164. Englewood Cliffs, New Jersey: Prentice-Hall, Inc., 1968.

Tuya, Manuel de. *Evangelio de San Lucas.* In *Biblia Comentada.* Vol. V. Madrid: Biblioteca de Autores Cristianos, 1971.

Gospel of John

Barrett, C. K. *The Gospel according to St. John.* London: William Clowes and Sons, 1962.

Bernard, John Henry. *A Critical and Exegetical Commentary on the Gospel according to St. John.* 2 Vols. In *The International Critical Commentary.* Reprint ed. Edinburgh: T. & T. Clark, 1958.

Bouyer, Louis. *Le quatrième Evangile.* Maredsous: Casterman, 1958.

Brown, Raymond E. *The Gospel according to John.* 2 Vols. In *The Anchor Bible.* Garden City, N.Y.: Doubleday, 1970.

Bultmann, Rudolf. *The Gospel of John. A Commentary.* Translated by G. R. Beasley-Murray, R. W. N. Hoare, and J. K. Riches. Philadelphia: The Westminster Press, 1971.

Bussche, Henri van den. *El Evangelio según San Juan.* Madrid: Ediciones Studium, 1972.

Carrillo Alday, Salvador. *El Evangelio de San Juan.* México: Instituto de Sagrada Escritura, 1978.

Durand, Alfred. *Evangelio según San Juan.* Madrid: Ediciones Paulinas, 1964.

Guichou, Pierre. *El Evangelio de San Juan.* Madrid: Ediciones Paulinas, 1964.

Hoskyns, Edwyn Clement. *The Fourth Gospel.* London: Faber and Faber Ltd., 1961.
Lagrange, Marie-Joseph. *Evangile selon Saint Jean.* Paris: J. Gabalda, 1948.
Leal, Juan. *Evangelio de San Juan.* In *La Sagrada Escritura Nuevo Testamento.* Vol. I. pp. 765–1107. Madrid: Biblioteca de Autores Cristianos, 1964.
Lightfoot, R. H. *St. John's Gospel.* Oxford: University Press, 1960.
Mollat, Donatien. *L'Evangile de Saint Jean.* Paris: Les Editions du Cerf, 1953.
Sanders, J. N. *A Commentary on the Gospel according to St. John.* In *Harper's New Testament Commentaries.* Edited by B. A. Mastin. New York: Harper & Row, 1969.
Schnackenburg, Rudolf. *Das Johannesevangelium.* Vols. I-II. Freiburg, Basel, Vienna: Herder, 1971.
Segalla, Giuseppe. *Giovanni.* Roma: Edizioni Paoline, 1976.
Vawter, Bruce. *The Gospel according to John.* In *The Jerome Biblical Commentary.* Vol. II. pp. 414–466. Englewood Cliffs, New Jersey: Prentice-Hall, Inc., 1968.
Wescott, Brooke Foss. *The Gospel according to St. John.* London: James Clarke & Co., 1958.
Wikenhauser, Alfred. *El Evangelio según San Juan.* Barcelona: Herder, 1967.

Acts of the Apostles

Boudou, A. *Los Hechos de los Apóstoles.* In *Verbum salutis.* Madrid: Ediciones Paulinas, 1964.
Bruce, F. F. "The Holy Spirit in the Acts of the Apostles." *Interpretation* 27 (1973), pp. 166–183.
Cerfaux, Lucien and Dupont, Jacques. *Les Actes des Apôtres.* Paris: Editions du Cerf, 1954.
Conzelmann, Hans. *Die Apostelgeschichte.* In *Handbuch zum Neuen Testament* 7. Tubingen: 1963.
Dillon, Richard J. and Fitzmyer, Joseph A. *Acts of the Apostles.* In *The Jerome Biblical Commentary.* Vol. II. pp. 165–214. Englewood Cliffs, New Jersey: Prentice-Hall, Inc., 1968.

Drumwright, H. L., Jr. "The Holy Spirit in the Book of Acts." *Southwestern Journal of Theology* 17 (1974), pp. 3–17.

Haenchen, Ernst. *The Acts of the Apostles. A Commentary.* Translated by B. Noble and G. Shinn. Philadelphia: Westminster, 1971.

Kürzinger, Josef. *Los Hechos de los Apóstoles.* Barcelona: Herder, 1974.

Leal, Juan. *Hechos de los Apóstoles.* Madrid: Biblioteca de Autores Cristianos, 1965.

Martini, Carlo M. *Atti degli Apostoli.* Roma: Edizioni Paoline, 1974.

Munck, Johannes. *The Acts of the Apostles.* Revised by W. F. Albright and C. S. Mann. In *The Anchor Bible.* Garden City, N.Y.: Doubleday, 1967.

Renie, J. *Actes des Apôtres.* In *La Bible Pirot-Clamer.* Paris: Letouzey et Ané, 1951.

Trocmé, E. *Le Livre des Actes et l'histoire.* Paris: 1957.

Turrado, Lorenzo. *Hechos de los Apóstoles.* Madrid: Biblioteca de Autores Cristianos, 1965.

Wikenhauser, Alfred. *Los Hechos de los Apóstoles.* Barcelona: Herder, 1967.

Williams, D. R. *Acts of the Apostles.* London: SCM Press, 1969.

Versions

La Biblia de Jerusalén. Bilbao: Desclée de Brouwer, 1975.

La traduction oecuménique de la Bible. Paris: Editions du Cerf—Les Bergers et les Mages, 1972.